MW00906738

Important Notice!

To the best of our knowledge, nobody reading this book has ever burst into flames or been struck on the head by a falling meteorite.

Nevertheless, it seems like it might be a good idea to wear a crash helmet and to have something on hand to quench flames - maybe a mug of beer.

I'm just saying...

What I've Learned... So Far

So Far

Part II:

Angels, Chimps & Tater Mitts

Mike Ball

What I've Learned... So Far
Part II: Angels, Chimps & Tater Mitts

Visit our Web site at
http://learnedsofar.com
for more information.

ISBN: 1-4751-1522-9

This book is dedicated to Mr. Remmo, my 8th grade football coach and English teacher. He beat the tar out of me on the football field, then stood and wept as he read one of my poems to the class .

I assume it was because he liked it.

Mr. Remmo changed the way I look at the craft of writing. He changed my understanding of what it means to be a strong man. He changed my life in ways he probably never knew, and in ways that I am just now beginning to understand.

Acknowledgements

I would like to take a few minutes to thank some people who were instrumental in helping me bring this book into the world:

My wife Nancy, who has spent nearly four decades listening to my half-baked ideas, laughing at my slightly more fully-baked jokes, tapping her foot to my guitar playing, bandaging my boo-boos, and cleaning up the wreckage after every one of my home improvement projects.

My son Patrick and his beautiful wife Shannon, who have to put up with me telling the world nearly as much about everything they do as they routinely publish on Facebook.

Scott Lorenz, my publicist, my strategic brain trust, and still the best friend I could ever hope to have.

My Editors, Yvonne Lorenz and Pamela Gossiaux, who are both apparently aware that it's "its," not "it's," when it's about its it-ness. At least I think it is.

And to all my readers, without whom there would be no point in writing this stuff.

Introduction

This is my second book, Part II of What I've Learned... So Far. As I send this off to press, it is early in the year 2012.

According to the ancient Mayans, a dragon is going to come around during this coming December and eat the Earth, or something like that. Of course, we might question the absolute accuracy of this prediction, since the ancient Mayans never saw it coming that they were all going to die from a combination of Conquistadors and chicken pox.

In any case, you should have plenty of time to enjoy this book, if you go ahead and get started with it.

A lot has happened since the publication, back in 2009, of my first book, *Bikes, Docks & Slush*

Nuggets. For one thing, I've grown a mostly-gray beard. I was going to grow a red or a black one, then I decided that it might make me look too much like a Viking raider, and that since I have almost completely given up pillaging European villages, I should probably go ahead with the gray. My son still thinks I just dozed off with my face in the mashed potatoes.

Perhaps even more important than the beard is the fact that my charity, Lost Voices, has gained a lot of momentum. We work with incarcerated and at-risk kids, helping them write and perform original music, trying to sort out the problems that got them in trouble in the first place. You will find several pieces in this book talking about Lost Voices and these really special kids. I would also encourage you to learn more at lostvoices.org.

Finally my band, Dr. Mike & The Sea Monkeys, has been working its way into the pantheon of folk music legend, to stand with performers like Tom "What The Hell Is The Next Chord" Peabody, and Carl "That Dude Has Crackers In His Beard" Wilson.

Through Lost Voices and the Sea Monkeys I've had the privilege of sharing real stages with real legends, like Josh White, Jr., Peter Madcat Ruth, Kitty Donohoe, Reverend Robert Jones, and a host of other massively talented people who have been kind enough to let me ride along in their musical wake. A CD of Sea Monkey Music will be coming along soon. You can keep in touch with this and other Sea Monkey Shenanigans at:

SeaMonkeyBand.com

or

Facebook.com/SeaMonkeyBand.

As always, I would love to hear from you:

LearnedSoFar.com

or

Facebook.com/MikeBallAuthor

or send an email to:

mike@learnedsofar.com

Enjoy the book!

The Extraordinary Discipline of a Serious Columnist

You know, I'll bet writing a column like this one looks like a pretty easy job. All you have to do is ramble on for a while about whatever you think needs rambling on about, crank out some jokes, and check it over to make sure that at least most of what you've written is English. Then you just pack your masterpiece off to the syndicate and bathe in the deep satisfaction of a job well done.

Well, I'm here to tell you that it's not always that easy. Like right now - the sun is shining, the birds are singing, and one of my friends just called me from his ski boat to see if I could come out to play. Of course, being the disciplined professional that I am…

Ok I'm back. I think I may have slightly strained a hamstring on that last set on the jump skis, so it actually feels kind of good to sit here at the computer and get my work done. After all, I have responsibilities. I simply have to ignore distractions like this other friend who just called me from his new boat to help him see if the racing engine he had installed will let us go faster than 90 MPH...

Ok, I'm back. I just have to catch my breath and polish the dead bugs off my glasses, then I can get down to business.

As I was saying, on days like this I have to rely on a strong work ethic to get my job done. It's kind of like that old fable of the ant, who worked hard to get ready for the winter, while the grasshopper just danced around and played the fiddle all day. As I recall the story, when winter came the ant was all cozy and well-fed, while the grasshopper was cold and hungry outside in the snow.

Of course, when spring rolled around the world's only fiddle-playing grasshopper signed a million-dollar recording contract, while the ant got fried by a third-grader with a magnifying glass.

But that's not the point. The point is, I have to maintain a high level of creative focus and intensity to deliver the kind of product my readers have come to expect. I've invested in a good laptop Mac, so I can sit on the deck and enjoy nice weather while I work. Being a seasoned pro, I have trained myself to shut out distractions like that pontoon boat full of friends who just pulled up to the dock and invited me to go out with them to taste-test Beers of All Nations. I simply have to politely but firmly tell them that I have work to do…

Ok, I'm bash. Bam. Bat. Back. That's it, backety-back-back. Hee, hee, hee. Who'd have known that beer could reflect such a rich cultural divers… div… so much cultural stuff. And stuff. But now I really have to get crankin' on the old column-poo, even though I could use a little nap…

Ok, I'm back. The bottom line of this whole thing is, to be a columnist you need to develop a steely resolve to make sure the job is done and done well, no matter what may be going on around you. Like right now, in response to this invitation to judge the Swedish Bikini Team Beach Volleyball Competition, I can conscientiously do a word count to see if I have enough…

The Story of Carlson the Pissed Off Angel

Carlson was not a particularly happy Angel. You see, he wasn't allowed to live in Heaven. He was a Guardian Angel, which meant that he had to hang around on Earth, taking care of his Client, Bob.

Now, Guardian Angel duty was about the most difficult job an Angel could have, even under the best of circumstances. Angels couldn't change what their Clients said or did; they could only try to protect them from accidents. Or, more commonly, from the consequences of their actions.

Some Clients were really good people, always risking their lives saving others, and this sort of thing could keep a Guardian Angel pretty busy. Other Clients were hopelessly slow-witted or accident prone, and they needed a Guardian Angel around constantly just to keep them from getting their scarves caught in the wood chipper.

Carlson was not sure why he had been assigned to Bob, who wasn't particularly accident prone, and who certainly wasn't what anybody would ever call a good person. Bob liked to steal books from the public library. He liked to harass waitresses without mercy, then leave a one-cent tip. And if you ever gave Bob a Christmas gift, you were likely to get it back the next year, slightly used and usually rewrapped in the same paper.

One night, just before Christmas, Carlson was pounding down a few nectars with his co-workers at the Angels' Holiday Office Party. He shook his head at the Angels standing around him and asked, "Why do you suppose the Boss wants me to take care of an idiot like Bob?"

"Maybe Bob has some hidden good qualities," said Boadicia. "Perhaps he is destined to do something wonderful."

"It's easy for you to see the good in people, Bo," said Trilium. "Your Client is going to be a saint someday. And mine is going to win the Nobel Peace Prize."

"Bob swipes change from blind beggars," said Carlson.

Fozitt shrugged sympathetically and said, "I'm

sure he really needs you. Maybe he… excuse me."
Fozitt looked at her pager and said, "I have to
go. My Client just decided to strike a match and
check for gas leaks by the furnace." She smiled,
shrugged again, and vanished.

At that moment Carlson's pager went off. "Oh
no," said Carlson, "Bob got in a fistfight with a
Salvation Army Santa, and now a mob is about
to tear him apart. I'll be back - save me a piece of
manna." He vanished too.

When Carlson got there, Bob was surrounded
by shouting men and women, holding them at
bay by swinging the donation kettle at them. The
Salvation Army Santa sat on the curb, his beard
dangling from a white elastic cord, holding a
handkerchief up to his bleeding nose.

Carlson spread his wings, and glanced around,
trying to decide what sort of distraction he could
create to give Bob a chance to escape. Then he
looked at Bob, at the bleeding Santa, and back at
Bob. "I can't take it any more," he shouted in the
general direction of Heaven. "Give me a break
here, Boss!"

At that moment Carlson caught sight of an
elderly woman standing quietly just outside the
ring of angry people. Tears were running down
her cheeks, and Carlson knew that she was
Bob's mother.

In the twenty-five years that Carlson had been on this assignment, he had never known Bob to visit his mother, to call her, or even to mention her. In fact it had never occurred to him that someone like Bob would even have a mother. Assuming human form, Carlson walked over to the woman. "Are you all right?" he asked gently.

The woman looked up at him and straightened her shoulders. "Yes," she sniffed, "Thank you." She nodded her head toward Bob. "Ever since he ran away from home twenty-five years ago, I've prayed that a Guardian Angel would watch over him and keep him safe. Now, here he is, and it looks like he just may not be worth it." She blinked as fresh tears welled up in her eyes. "But I can't help it. He's my son."

Carlson nodded slowly, then closed his eyes and waved his right hand. The crowd, the bleeding Santa, and the donation bucket all disappeared, leaving just Bob, his mother, and Carlson standing on the deserted street corner. "Go ahead," Carlson whispered, fading from her sight and from her memory. "Talk to him."

She stared, puzzled, at the air where Carlson had been. Then, heading toward her bewildered son, she called out, "Bobby?"

Carlson hovered near the street lamp and watched them. When he saw Bob take his mother in his arms, both of them shaking with sobs, he smiled and looked up at Heaven.

"I get it now, Boss," he said. "You should have told me that I work for his mom."

Welcome to the Conspicuous Consumption Club!

I just got back from my weekly trip to Costco.

I borrowed a furniture dolly from a neighbor so I could haul my 200-roll *Convenience Pack* of toilet paper, my thirty pound *Family Pack* of chicken wings, my six-cubic-yard *Do-It-Yourself Landfill* bag of potting soil, and my twenty-five gallon *You Must Be An Idiot Bucket 'O Hot Sauce* in from the car.

God, I love Costco!

"Warehouse" shopping clubs have become a way of life for a lot of people. The concept is fairly simple; you build a huge, open building with a high ceiling and a cement floor, fill it with big shelves loaded with institutional-sized packages of pretty much anything a person might possibly want to buy, and let the shoppers fight it out for themselves. You do all your merchandising with a forklift.

And you charge a membership fee. This keeps the riff-raff out. After all, who wants to mix with the sort of people who don't appreciate the value of buying their mayonnaise or tube socks by the hundredweight?

One of the key features that makes Costco work is the variety of merchandise available. In the old days, our ancestors would have had to go to three different stores to get donuts, dress shirts, and car batteries. Can you imagine the inconvenience?

At Costco, a single guy planning a big evening with the girlfriend can buy some flowers, a DVD of that movie she's been wanting to see, a gallon of Captain Morgan, a pack of condoms, and an economy-sized box of Alka-Seltzer for the next morning.

Why, the organized smoker can buy cigarettes, health insurance, and a coffin, all in one easy shopping trip!

Of course, the best thing about Costco is the food samples. Scattered throughout the store they have ladies in hairnets and plastic gloves cooking steak bits and baby back ribs, dipping ice cream, and pouring Mango nectar. Shoppers can, and do, literally graze the store for a free meal. This is not without its down side. Sample stations giving away the really good stuff can create feeding frenzies that bring store traffic to a standstill.

These feeding frenzies also produce distracted drivers, those guilt-driven individuals who push their carts away from the sample stations with one hand while they shove pizza-bagel-bits into their mouths with the other. They smack their lips, make "yummy" noises, and gaze skyward, attempting to con the sample lady into believing that they are deep in the throes of a difficult purchasing decision, then run broadside into another lip-smacking distracted driver whose cart has the *Modular Redwood Backyard Play Set (One Full Redwood Included)* balanced on top of the *Make All The Kids In Your Neighborhood Diabetic* freightload of Yoo-hoo.

Now personally, I prefer Costco over its chief rival, whose name rhymes with Schmam's Blub. At that place, affiliated with a company whose name rhymes with Schmalmart, I find the cracking whips, the jangling manacles, and the soul-searing screams of the employees to be kind of distracting.

So here I sit surrounded by my most recent Costco plunder, gazing with warm affection at my brand new 64-pack of nine volt batteries. You see, I had to replace the battery in the smoke detector last week. That's the first time I've seen one of those little rectangular devils in a couple of years – in fact, since the last time I replaced the battery in the smoke detector.

Just thought I'd better stock up.

The End of a Bad Seed.

Who'd have thought good crops
Could come from a bad seed?

It was a pretty good line in a really good poem, entitled "Look At Me," by a seventeen year old African-American poet named Donald. This young man was theoretically every bit as dangerous as he was gifted; he was incarcerated in the WJ Maxey Boys Training School as a violent offender.

I was working with Donald on a documentary called "Young Poet Incarcerated," helping him polish some of his work and rehearse it before we rolled the camera. We had been given some money by the National Endowment for the Arts through the Michigan Humanities Council and the Michigan Council for Arts and Cultural Affairs to cover some of the costs of making our movie.

The idea of the film was to let Donald use his poetry to give the world a glimpse into how a kid gets himself locked up before he's old enough to vote.

As with all of Donald's work, there were some other powerful lines in that poem;

No cradles, no cribs
I was born in a casket
Living to die
Though I survived among the savages.

or

There is a rose
But with their eyes closed
All they grabbing
Is thorns.

But as we worked our way through each line of "Look At Me," my mind kept wandering back to those words;

Who'd have thought good crops
Could come from a bad seed?

Finally I asked him, "Donald, are you telling me that you are a bad seed?"

"Oh, yes," he said, "I always been bad."

"All your life?"

"All my life."

"You were born that way? A bad seed?"

"Yeah. I been bad all my life."

"So you're telling me that a little baby is born evil."

"Oh no, a baby is born in the image of God..." He stopped and looked down at the floor. "Oh."

"I think maybe that line needs a little work."

"I guess so." And then we went on to work on another poem.

A week later Donald and I were working together again, and we made our way back around to "Look At Me." This time he pulled out and unfolded a different piece of paper than the one he had been using. "I did like you said. I did some work on this since last week."

"Let's hear it."

And he began to read. When he got to the "bad seed" line he paused and looked up at me, and then kept reciting, giving me the new line from memory.

> *Who'd have thought good crops*
> *Could come from a bad seed?*
> *Never a bad seed*
> *Only bad dirt.*

It is fairly common these days for people to compliment me for the work I do with the kids. When this happens, I always feel kind of embarrassed, and find myself struggling to find ways to explain to them that I simply feel blessed to have the skills I have, and to get the opportunity to put all those gifts to use like this.

I only wish that I could let them in on exactly what it was like when Donald spoke those words and smiled, looking at me through eyes that were at once seventeen and a thousand years old. If those people could feel what I felt in that moment, I would never have to explain a thing.

You can see the entire mini-documentary, Young Poet Incarcerated, online at http://lostvoices.org.

2008 – The Year in Preview

I don't know about you, but as this year draws to its choking, sputtering conclusion, I am getting just a little bit tired of all the "retrospectives" that are clogging up the media. We've read about best and worst movies of 2007. We've read about the best and worst people, the best and worst moments, the best and worst books, and the best and worst songs. I even saw an article about the Ten Best and Worst News Articles of the Year - it came in at number seven on the Worst list.

I prefer to look ahead, to peer into my unfailingly accurate crystal ball and predict the future. Unfortunately, since I recently traded the crystal ball for a harmonica, I'll just have to wing it. So here it is, my 2008 Year in Preview.

January, 2008 – CNN commentator Lou Dobbs announces a breakthrough in the combined fields of recycling and immigration reform. He asks all Americans to collect their holiday fruitcakes and, instead of saving them to re-gift next year, to send them to the U.S. Border Patrol where they will be used to build a Wall that will keep Mexicans from crossing our borders and taking our jobs. After the plan is implemented, it turns out that Mexicans love fruitcake. The Wall is gone within a few hours, and Dobbs' head explodes.

February, 2008 - After an intense nation-wide search, a reporter from the New Republic locates the last person on the planet who still thinks that George W. Bush was a pretty darned good choice for president. Clyde Delusion of Crow Butte, Texas, a professional survivalist and part-time cattle rustler, states that Bush is a lot better than that "… rich, faggy, East Coast John Kerry guy." He goes on to say, "Mr. Bush is 'specially good for our country, on account of he's a real, red-blooded man's man, and a true son of Texas." Informed that Bush is actually from New Haven, Connecticut and was a cheerleader at his prep-school in Andover Massachusetts, Mr. Delusion's head explodes.

April, 2008 - Britney Spears, Paris Hilton, and Lindsay Lohan will get together to form a new joint venture. The company, "21st Century Skank, Ltd," will design and promote a line of cocaine-based cosmetics, and (at Britney's insistence) hair-care products. After sampling their products, all three girls' heads explode.

June, 2008 - Bill O'Reilly meets an untimely end while debating American foreign policy on The Factor with Rosemont Junior College freshman Amy Nosebleed. When O'Reilly is unable to shout loudly enough to drown out Miss Nosebleed's statement that there is really no proof that all Democrats are Nazi sympathizers, he accidentally cuts off his own microphone rather than hers. She is able to make her point on the air, and O'Reilly's head explodes.

August, 2008 - Sacha Baron Cohen, who recently retired his misogynistic, anti-Semitic character "Borat," creates a new character, "Churchrat." This new satirical character is an ultra right-wing gay-bashing Christian preacher, who is also a blatant embezzler and a gay pedophile. When Cohen learns that his newly-created Church of the Divine Diddler has become the fastest-growing religious organization in America, his head explodes.

October, 2008 - Just before the November Presidential Election, George W. Bush declares martial law, then appoints himself "Decider-Guy For Life." With the exception of Justices Clarence Thomas and Antonin Scalia, the entire United States Supreme Court's heads explode.

December, 2008 - Newly appointed Vice President For Life Dick Cheney officially has his name changed to "Caligula" and breaks ground on a gigantic Coliseum to house a "… new age of glorious gladiatorial combat and human sacrifice." To Cheney's deep disappointment, nobody is particularly surprised, and not one single head explodes.

So there's the year ahead, all laid out so you can plan accordingly. If nothing else, you might want to pick up a slicker and a pair of goggles. And remember, if anything I've predicted here actually happens, it will be news to me.

Happy New Year!

Tweet Me! Tweet Me Good!

I just got a "Tweet" from Barack Obama - me and 111, 829 of his closest friends. Make that 111,831; two more people started "Following" him while I was writing the previous sentence. Whoops, 111,837.

And twelve minutes ago I found out that Maggie Mason in San Francisco (8,127 Followers) doesn't get much exercise in "the muscles you use to whip your head from side to side when dancing with tequila in hand."

You gotta love the twenty-first century!

If none of this makes any sense at all to you, join the crowd. What I'm talking about here is an online service called "Twitter," the latest way for anybody with internet access and a cell phone to keep the world posted on how awesome you think Heidi Klum's Halloween costume was.

The way it works is whenever the mood strikes, you post a short text message to your Twitter page. As soon as you do that, anyone who has decided to Follow you gets this valuable information on their own Twitter page and on their cell phone.

I found out about Twitter a few weeks ago when I went to a presentation by a public relations expert who was talking about the latest ways people talk to each other. Once I got over the fact that this guy, who is clearly at the peak of success in his profession, was a good deal younger than the shoes I was wearing, his ideas began to sink in.

It turns out that, at least as far as ideas go, the world has shrunk so much that you can carry it around in your pocket with your car keys and Rolaids. You can communicate with anybody, anywhere, any time you feel like it. Eight seconds ago "mazui" told "romp:"

"次会う時まで持っててもらっていい？ じつかねさんの画像まだ捜し中"

I guess that settles that! I'm almost completely sure mazui's post has nothing whatsoever to do with carrot cake, a crash helmet, and a jar of Vaseline.

Of course, to most professional writers the internet is the greatest thing since cold beer. Years ago I would finish typing the final draft of a piece, slide it into an envelope, scrounge around for enough postage stamps to get it where it had to go, then sit back and crack myself a cold one. It would be at least a couple of weeks before I got any sort of feedback.

Now I can hit the "save" button when I post a column, and have a comment from a reader in Indonesia before I have a chance to get a thumbnail under the pop top.

And unless you've been living in a Turkish prison for the last few years, you are probably familiar with the concept of "blogs," where someone who is not necessarily (or even remotely) a writer can maintain an online commentary for anyone who is interested in hot topics like Siamese cats (as of today there are 37,752 Siamese cat blogs), boogers (59,781) or cheesecake (631,700).

This Twitter thing is a little bit different. For one thing, you have to pretty much get right to the point with what you have to say. Because they are meant to hit cell phones as text messages, each "Tweet" consists of a maximum of 140 characters, including spaces and punctuation. Here is a maxed-out Tweet:

"The challenge we all face is to keep our breakfast cereal free of St. Bernard droppings. It goes without saying; or at least it should have."

So now I have a way to instantly keep track of Barack Obama's campaign stops, the latest international headlines, or the outcome of this morning's bagel run by Biz Stone in Berkley (2 salt, 2 garlic, 2 everything).

Now I just need to figure out why I like Twitter so darned much.

Gee Honey, Your Hair Smells Like Victory

I was just sitting here wondering why any woman would want her hair to smell like pomegranate.

OK, I admit this is a sure sign that I would probably be way better off if I spent less time thinking. And many people would argue that I might do well to think about more important things, like the effect of near-light speed on gravitational forces, or about possible causes and cures for Restless Leg Syndrome.

But I can't help it. I'm kind of stuck with the brain I've got, and right now it's speculating on why women might want to use hair care products that leave them smelling like they have fruit salad on their heads. I feel safe in assuming that it is not to impress men, because most guys prefer things that smell like food to be - well, food.

And besides, the food scents that attract men are things like beer, French fries, and anything cooking on a grill. Have you ever seen a shampoo that cleans, conditions, and smells like bratwurst?

In the interest of solid scientific research, I decided to call my friend Megan and ask her what she's thinking about whenever she visits the hair care aisle.

Me: So, what are you thinking about whenever you visit the hair care aisle?

Megan: I'm thinking I don't want my hair to smell like guys' hair.

Me: Really? What does guys' hair smell like?

Megan: Feet.

Me:

Megan: Or worse.

Me:

Megan: Of course, I also want my hair to smell better than the other girls'.

Me: Why? Women aren't really all that competitive, are they?

Megan:

Me: So most guys smell like feet?

Megan: Or worse.

Me: Yet you like guys.

Megan: Sure.

Me: What about guys who wear way too much cologne?

Megan: I assume they either own a party store or they're gay.

Me: How about those commercials where the nerdy guy uses the body spray and then gets attacked by hundreds of beautiful sex-crazed girls?

Megan: Something like that would never happen. Those hot girls wouldn't swarm a guy like that if he sprayed himself with hundred dollar bills.

Me: They wouldn't?

Megan: Nope. For one thing, they'd be too busy talking about each others' outfits.

Me: That makes sense. I guess.

Megan: Plus, can you imagine the smells in that body pile? Every one of the girls would be wearing their own shampoo, conditioner, bath oil, perfume, cologne, and whatever else. There's nothing you could put on a guy that would overcome all that.

Me: So I wasted my money buying five cases of that body spray?

Megan:

So there you have it. This detailed psychographic research proves that women mainly want to smell good so that they can claim victory over other women, that guys can't really get away with smelling like anything other than feet, and that bratwurst might smell better to a guy than a pomegranate, but it would never wind up in a best-selling shampoo.

I think I'll go take a shower.

What Ever Happened to Crappy Kid Cars?

Driving by the high school parking lot last week, I was struck by the fact that every vehicle sitting out there could be clearly and easily distinguished from a pile of scrap metal. Most of them were newer than the car I drive. A few were newer than the oil in the car I drive.

What's up with that?

My first car was a 1961 Buick LeSabre. I paid $50 for it, more than two months' take-home from my job washing dishes in a family restaurant. The car was big – the front and back bumpers were nearly always in different zip codes. It had a huge V8 engine, but since it weighed slightly more than a truckload of bulldozers, it wasn't very fast. Of course, every day I drove my Buick it got a little bit lighter, as bits of trim and apparently unneeded engine parts fell off.

I have never had, nor do I expect ever to have, a possession that I loved more.

My Buick was two-toned when I got it – beige and rust. The first thing I did was wash more dishes, save up another couple of months' pay, slap a little Bondo into the rust holes, and take my Buick down for a $49.95 paint job. It was not lost on me that the car was worth exactly one nickel more than the paint.

The new color I chose was a sort of leprechaun-on-an-acid-trip green, so my friends immediately co-opted the Simon and Garfunkel song and named my car the "Big Bright Green Pleasure Machine." This was a tribute to the fact that we could go just about anywhere with eight kids stuffed into the big bench seats. For trips to the drive-in movie, we could pack another two or three (four or five if they were girls and had skipped supper) in the trunk.

After a few more mountains of clean dishes, I treated the BBGPM to the ultimate touch of class: an eight-track tape player, mounted in the glove box so passers-by wouldn't covet it and be tempted to steal it, along with two massive black surface-mount speakers screwed to the rear deck. If you turned the volume and the bass all the way up, you could use the vibrations from In-A-Gadda-Da-Vida to liquefy a cheerleader.

The Big Bright Green Pleasure Machine burned a lot of gas, but back then gas was cheap – even for a guy grossing eighty cents an hour. It also burned a lot of oil, so we carried a case of 10W-40 in the trunk, and we were always followed by a friendly trail of blue smoke. During the hundred thousand miles I put on that car, I never got around to replacing the tires.

The engine sang with a deep, throaty growl, owing to the fact that the exhaust system had been entirely replaced by "muffler bandages" and duct tape wrapped around the remnants of rusted pipes and baffles. A beer can jammed behind the left headlight held it in place, since any metal in the area that could possibly hold a screw (or duct tape) had mysteriously disintegrated.

As I looked across the shining ranks of twenty-first century kid cars outside the high school, all of them with treads on the tires and fully-functioning head lights, I had a vision of the Big Bright Green Pleasure Machine rumbling into that parking lot, loaded with eight kids (since we weren't going to the drive-in theater) and smoking like a crop duster, with Iron Butterfly shaking the sheet metal. And I could not help wondering if these kids with their comfortable, reliable rides might just be missing something.

Nah.

Does Anybody Know a "Guy Hollerin?"

Many years ago, when I was a creative director in the advertising business, my team had the opportunity to create the theme for a new restaurant. We wanted it to be sports-oriented, but we were trying for something a little bit different from the standard hot-wings-and-a-pitcher-while-you-watch-the-big-game sports bar.

It was a Friday when I discovered that our client was about to buy a pre-fabricated family bar/restaurant package, apparently a fairly standard 1980's BenniFriApplChiligans menu with a clever assortment of antique wagon wheels and pitchforks to hang on the wall. I had somehow managed to convince them to give me one week to show them a better concept.

I knew that it would take my artists, turbocharged as they were with Snickers bars and Mountain Dew, every bit of five days to create the artwork I would need for the client pitch. This meant that I had the weekend to come up with some sort of idea.

I had to let the restaurant problem roll around in the back of my mind though, because the really important item on that Saturday's agenda was my seven-year-old son's first experience with ice hockey. My wife had signed him up for the Spring Recreational Hockey League while I was out of town. This had come as something of a surprise to me, since;

a.) it happened at the same time we were refinancing the house to put braces on his teeth, and;

b.) to my knowledge the only time our son had ever been on ice skates was when he was about four and he spent an hour hanging onto a traffic cone in the middle of the rink in a "Toddlers On Ice" skating class.

I took the video camera along to the rink, so that I could record the historic first strides of my future Conn Smythe Trophy winner. I ran exactly 27 seconds of tape before I shut the camera off out of sheer mercy to the angst-ridden and self-conscious adult my son would someday become.

You see, that hour hanging onto the traffic cone had unaccountably failed to turn him into a masterful skater. So while all the other kids, who had obviously logged a bit more traffic cone time, rocketed up and down the ice, my son clutched his brand new hockey stick and hobbled around like a penguin on a pool table.

As I watched, I started adding up the damage; helmet $65, shoulder pads $40, gloves $65, pants $35, skates $85, elbow pads $15, shin guards $15, mouth guard $25, hockey bag $35, lime green hockey tape, lime green skate laces, and Detroit Red Wings water bottle $20…

Afterward, sitting in the truck on the way home, my son was very quiet for a while. Then he broke the silence with, "Dad, it's really embarrassing that I can't keep up with any of those other kids…" and I silently prepared to kiss a $400 investment in hockey gear goodbye.

"So," he continued, "I'm going to really have to work hard to catch up. Will you take me skating this afternoon?"

And at that instant I knew what to do with that restaurant. We would make it a sports bar based on the exploits of a fictional World's Greatest Athlete. But our hero would not be the greatest because he was bigger, stronger, more genetically gifted, or more chemically altered than all the rest.

Our hero would be a small, unassuming guy who would be the greatest athlete in the world simply because it never occurred to him not to be.

The following Monday, my team and I created a character named Guy Hollerin (the illustrator came up with the name). Guy is a skinny blonde fellow who wears a red, white, and blue sweat band, and oversized aviator eyeglasses. For the menu and restaurant décor, we created a detailed legend around Guy's exploits in every possible field of sport.

We got the account, and now, nearly twenty years later, Guy Hollerin's is a fine sports restaurant and bar on the north side of Ann Arbor. But almost nobody has any idea that there is a real Guy Hollerin. He's a little seven-year-old who once rode home next to me in his brand new hockey gear.

And figured out exactly what it takes to conquer the world.

Wedding Bells and Chocolate Pudding

We went to a wedding today. The bride was the daughter of a couple who have been our friends for more than thirty years. Looking at this radiant drop-dead gorgeous young woman in her wedding dress, beaming at the handsome young man who was the love of her life, I couldn't escape the vision of chocolate pudding smeared on the cheeks of a four-year-old little girl who used to light up rooms with that exact same sun-breaking-through-clouds smile.

We had never met the young man who found himself at the center of this whole operation. In the slide presentation at the reception we did get to see a photograph of him taken a few years back, in which he was walking away from the camera, holding a sippy cup in one hand and what appeared to be a stuffed weasel in the other, and clearly enjoying a little "naked time."

His parents had obviously discovered that the secret of dealing with naked little boys is making sure their hands are full.

We learned a little more from the toast of the best man, who stopped just short of telling us that the groom's Animal House name was "Bluto." Then there was the toast by the groom's father, who seemed genuinely amazed to see his son clothed, much less in a tuxedo.

This is the stuff of weddings. Since the dawn of civilization we humans have developed elaborate rituals to mark the day when we pack the kids off to enjoy their very own joint tax return. For instance, in ancient Roman weddings, a thin loaf of bread was broken over the couple's heads, a tradition reflected today in the shoving of wedding cake up the bride's nose.

The Chinese Wedding Album is a feature of many modern Chinese (imagine that!) weddings. This is an elaborate collection of photographs of the bride and groom in a variety of different locations and costumes. We can assume that all of the pictures are numbered for the benefit of Americans who can't pronounce the captions.

In the Hindu wedding tradition, a turnip represents fulfillment and a happy marriage. In these parts the turnip signifies a beef pasty.

Which brings us to the wedding feast. I'm pretty sure that this has been around since Oog cracked a saber tooth tiger on the head and barbecued it for his daughter Oogella's wedding. And I wouldn't be one bit surprised to learn that Oog's brother-in-law got into a little too much grog and passed out on the pile of gift-wrapped stoneware (made from real… never mind).

Of course one of the most familiar and universal wedding customs is music at the reception, provided by either a live band or a DJ. In either case, in addition to playing "The Bunny Hop" and "Mony Mony," it is the entertainer's job to keep the party going and to make sure that the couple perform important rituals like the Garter Exchange, in which the wedding party at large gets a good view of the bride's underpants. In New Testament times, when the wedding celebration lasted a full seven days, just imagine how much material a Judean DJ must have had to come up with!

In the end, though, I think that the cakes, the garters, the Bunny Hop, and the brother-in-law sleeping it off among the monogrammed chafing dishes are all just nature's way of helping us parents work through the realization that, when it comes to our kids, we can't keep pudding on their faces and stuffed weasels in their hands forever.

They have to move on to pudding and stuffed weasels of their own.

A Brief History of Christmas

O Holy night, the stars are brightly shining.
It is the night of our dear Savior's birth.

A soft coating of pure white snow blankets the countryside. Stars twinkle in the cold winter sky. The welcome-home aroma of wood smoke drifts from my neighbor's chimney. Somewhere in the neighborhood, cookies shaped like angels are just coming out of the oven. Santa is finishing up his last couple of shifts at the mall, and all my credit cards are toast.

Christmas is here at last!

In the spirit of the season, I thought it would be fun to take a quick look at how MasterCard's favorite holiday came to be what it is today.

First off, it is pretty certain that December 25 is not really when Christ was born. In fact, we probably don't even have the year right. The best guess of Bible scholars is that he would more likely have been born on September 29, in the year 5 BC. That, or maybe sometime in March, a month which is considered holy among many people to the present day, as commemorated by the NCAA basketball tournament.

The reason we're not real sure is that the early Christians did not seem to think that details like Jesus' birthday were all that important in the big picture, probably because they were pretty busy getting fed to lions. Then along came the Emperor Constantine, who made Christianity the official religion of the Civilized World, and after that they were all busy feeding non-Christians to lions.

In about the middle of the 5th century the lions apparently got full, and so they had a little time to turn their attention to celebrating the birth of Jesus. The Pope at the time, Saint Sixtus III, decided to declare December 25 the official date for "Christ Mass," mostly because it coincided with the ancient Roman holiday of Saturnalia, and a lot of people were already used to taking that day off work.

In northern Europe and Scandinavia, the date marked a Norse holiday called "Yule," which roughly translates as "December is about the crappiest time of the year around here, and if you go outside your breath makes icicles on your upper lip, so we might as well all hang around indoors, burn a big log, roast a reindeer, and get really, really drunk."

A lot of our Christmas traditions come down to us from these pagan holidays; Christmas trees, mistletoe, holly, wreaths, caroling, exchanging gifts, peppermint schnapps, gaining 15 pounds in two weeks, and many others.

For hundreds of years the whole Christmas thing worked out pretty well, and people got right into the spirit. In fact, the revelry sometimes got so enthusiastic that it lead to the joyful burning of ghettos, public buildings, and, since lions had become relatively scarce, the occasional non-believer.

Then along came the Protestant Reformation. Among other things, the Protestants decided that wild celebrations and a bunch of customs with their roots in paganism were not fitting ways to celebrate the birth of the Savior. So they did the only thing they could - they spent a good part of the next three hundred years killing or being killed by people who didn't agree with their idea of the proper way to worship the Prince of Peace.

Among the Puritans of Colonial New England, Christmas celebrations and decorations were outlawed. It took more than two hundred years for these prohibitions to relax and for the old traditions to reassert themselves throughout America. It was not until 1870, when President Ulysses S. Grant discovered that the eggnog had rum in it, that Christmas became a national holiday.

Christmas as we know it today has evolved a great deal over the course of the twentieth century. A lot of our modern traditions have strong roots in commercial marketing, from the red-suited Santa Claus (popularized by an illustrator named Haddon Sundblom in a series of Coca Cola ads in the 1930s) to Rudolph the Red-Nosed Reindeer (who first appeared in a Montgomery Ward promotional book by a staff copy writer named Robert May). It seems that in our world, wherever there's a buck to be made, you will find a heartwarming Christmas character.

And to be honest, I don't really care. I treasure the memory of being about seven years old, lying in bed on Christmas eve and struggling to fall asleep so that I could take the "Sleepy-Eye Express to Christmas Morning." Then I could race downstairs and shred the wrapping paper from the cardboard cylinder of Lincoln Logs that had been sitting there under the tree, tormenting me.

I loved Rudolph, Frosty, Santa, and all the rest. I still do. And I loved making all that fun happen, to the extent I was able, for my son. Now when I see the lights on the Christmas tree, they remind me fondly of the absolute joy of unbridled childhood avarice.

But, despite the fact that the date and all the details may not be quite accurate, those lights also remind me of stars in the sky over a manger somewhere in the Middle East, where a little baby had no crib for a bed. A little baby who grew up to be the Savior of Mankind.

A Few Random Thoughts About the Holidays

Every year about this time I get to spend some quality time with Santa Claus, taking the official photographs of the Right Jolly Old Elf's encounters with terrified four-year-olds and their stressed-out mothers (who still have to get the kids to ballet class and hockey practice, plus figure out where to pick up a spiral sliced ham and something nice for their husband's secretary, but first they need to get a decent Santa shot for that way-past-deadline Family Newsletter).

• Every picture I snap represents a micro-documentary dealing with hopes, dreams, fears, fantasy, avarice, redemption, and the human condition. That, and the effects of a leaky diaper on red velvet pants.

• Some holiday cookies are so sweet that they actually make my head hurt.

• Eggnog is the best stuff ever. Always be sure to sprinkle a little nutmeg on top. And if you add a bit of rum, you will stay nice and warm if you should decide to, say, liven up the old office party by dancing your interpretation of the Nutcracker Ballet outside in the snow wearing nothing but your Rudolph The Red-Nosed Reindeer boxer shorts and a pair of clip-on antlers.

• I still write out a Christmas Wish List. For the past couple of years, I have sent an email to the North Pole. Now, I just found out that I can Twitter Santa!

• I have never met a Jewish, Muslim or other non-Christian person who actually got angry about being on the receiving end of a well-intentioned "Merry Christmas." That said, it seems like a pretty simple matter of common courtesy to say something, like "Happy Holidays," that would include everyone.

This is why I always wrote off the whole "War On Christmas" deal as just one more symptom of Bill O'Reilly's narcissistic personality disorder. Learning that the idea actually originated with (and is vigorously advocated by) a white supremacist group called VDare makes the whole issue a lot more disturbing.

• Whatever happened to tinsel? I miss it.

• I wonder how many grandchildren will receive "Barack Obama Collector Coin Sets" for Christmas this year, with cheek-pinching advice from Grandpa to "put them away to pay for college someday." After all, each coin is "layered in 24k pure gold." Not to be a wet blanket here, but I'd just like to point out that you could have a parking lot full of Hummers layered in 24k pure gold for about $1.35. In fact, that's not a bad idea. It beats driving them…

• The new LED Christmas lights are cool and futuristic. It's kind of like ripping the guts out of R2D2 and decorating your tree with them.

• There is a house near here owned by a guy who has to be the High Priest of Inflatable Holiday Decorations. At least I assume it's a guy, because no woman I've ever known would spend the kind of money we're talking about on things that you can't wear to a dinner party.

He celebrates every holiday in the year by filling his yard with cool seasonal stuff, complete with spot lighting and thematic groupings. This year, in addition to the normal array of blow-up snowmen, Santa sleighs and manger scenes, he has added a couple of life-sized inflatable deer standing on their hind legs, dressed in camo and holding what are presumably Remington Hunter-

Hunting rifles - a cute but vaguely disturbing sight. This may be because the existence of real armed deer would spell true economic disaster in Michigan, marking the decimation of the local Budweiser and Slim Jim industries.

Well, there is now just a little more than a week left for us to feel financially inadequate about Christmas. Cheer up, we're all in the same boat – just keep bailing.

Paris Hilton's Christmas List

What do you suppose Paris Hilton wants for Christmas?

I recently read in the New York Post (sometimes I like to go slumming – what can I say?) that the girl who is Famous For Being Famous just wants "… a man to fall in love with, one for life. Someone that I can start a family with."

Of course right around the same time as Paris made this comment, she was running around the clubs of Europe with no underpants and a variety of boy-toys, then posing for a new wine ad wearing nothing but a coat of gold latex and a few paint-roller marks. Sometimes it's hard to take her seriously.

Paris is almost the same age as my son, so I called him up and asked his opinion. "If I woke up on Christmas morning and discovered that I was Paris Hilton," he said, "I'd want a handgun. And one bullet. And instructions covering which end of the gun to put up against my head." Apparently he's not a real big Paris Hilton fan.

I guess nobody else I asked was a big fan either, since they all had pretty much the same answer - except for one person who said she would want an extra bullet "as a kindness to that creepy little dog."

So what exactly do you wrap up under the tree for a girl who gets paid $50,000 (plus an extra $10,000 for not wearing any underpants) just to show up at a bar mitzvah?

Of course there are the usual ultra-expensive gifts - things like toothpicks made from mastodon ivory, or diamond-encrusted iPhones - but I'd be surprised if our little Paris didn't already have most of that stuff. I'd even bet that if you dumped out her $45,000 Louis Vuitton handbag you'd find a tube of Guerlain lipstick, with its solid 18K gold case, 2.5 carats of diamonds, and a price tag of $62,000.

You could go all out and buy Paris a 253 mph Bugatti Veyron automobile for a little over two million dollars, or an 82-foot Bay SonShip Motor Yacht for just under five million, but she'd probably just return them for store credit.

For a bargain $1,764,000 you could book passage for Paris and five of her closest friends into space on the Burt Rutan-designed Virgin Galactic SpaceShipTwo. The bad news is that the next available flight will be... someday. That, and they don't offer a one-way option.

I guess, looking at all this from her point of view, Paris might have at least partly meant what she said about wanting someone to start a family with. She would probably find it a pretty nice change of pace to wake up next to a man and know his real name.

Better yet, I'll bet that she would like to wake up next to someone who knows exactly how she liked her coffee. Someone who will endure the frantic way she scrapes her ice cream dish at the end of the ice cream. Someone who thinks it is kind of cute when she snores, and who is grateful that she is willing to put up with him when he does.

Someone who will look at her thirty years from now and, even if she doesn't spend her weight in platinum every year on cosmetic surgery, still see the girl he sees today.

You know, I really hope that Paris eventually does find someone to spend her life with, although it seems to me that she is probably not really looking in the best places to find him. In the meantime - and I think that just about everyone will agree with me on this - there is one thing that I would really, really like to see Paris Hilton get for Christmas this year.

Underpants.

Happy Holidays, Bill O'Reilly

Boy, did I ever screw up the other day. I said, "Happy Holidays" to a Bill O'Reilly Fan. Lucky for me, this particular BORF was kind enough to immediately point out the error of my ways.

BORF: Happy Holidays? Tell me, why do you hate Jesus so much?

Me: What?

BORF: You've joined the leftist, Democrat, tax-and-spend liberal war on Christmas, so you must hate Jesus.

Me: I don't hate Jesus.

BORF: Then why are you mounting your secular assault on Christmas and trying to eliminate all that is holy in America?

Me: I'm not mounting anything. All I said was, "Happy Holidays."

BORF: Exactly! So you obviously want to destroy Christianity in our country.

Me: No I don't. In fact, it just so happens that I am a Christian.

BORF: What kind of Christian would say something like "Happy Holidays?" Why, you ought to be burned at the stake for that.

Me: Or crucified?

BORF: Exactly! What kind of Christian are you to do something that would, in a perfect world, get you crucified?

Me: The Catholic kind?

BORF: Aarggh! You see?

Me: Not really. So how exactly does saying "Happy Holidays" threaten Christianity?

BORF: Well, the way I heard it when I was just a little baby, every time somebody says "Happy Holidays," the cross sewn on the front of some real American's hooded white robe falls off. You can see how that would eventually destroy us all.

Me: Wow, I think I'm beginning to understand.

BORF: Darned right! We want everyone to embrace Christian values. The good kind. You know, "Do unto others before they try to do it unto you…"

Me: I think you might have that just a little bit wrong.

BORF: That's the way I learned it.

Me: Right. So what about non-Christians?

BORF: You mean like Catholics?

Me: Actually, I was thinking more of Jews, Muslims, Buddhists, or Hindus. Or even atheists.

BORF: They can all fend for themselves. Or go back where they came from. And you know where all the atheists can go!

Me: I guess so. You know, I'm pretty sure I read somewhere that Bill O'Reilly was born and raised Catholic.

BORF: Impossible. And even if he was once, he's better now. He's a Registered Independent, not some kind of rotten Papist.

Me: Again, my mistake. So, thanks for straightening me out on all of this.

BORF: No problem. It was the least I could do. And Merry Christmas!

Me: Feliz Navidad!

Ask Dr. Mike – Fruitcakes and the Holiday Pilgrimage

From time to time my readers, apparently not aware of my carefully cultivated lack of any useful knowledge whatsoever, write in and ask me to help them solve the important issues in their lives. This is one of those times. So, here is the new year's first action-packed installment of "Ask Dr. Mike."

Dear Dr. Funny Guy,

We are a young married couple, and my wife and I have just finished the annual holiday pilgrimage to spend time with all of our relatives.

What an ordeal! We were on the road so long that when we got back we found squatters living in our house. The squatters painted the kitchen and retiled the bathroom while we were gone, and they bought a great new couch for the family room, so we've asked them to stay.

Our problem is that even after all the visits, none of our relatives seemed completely satisfied. My wife's Uncle Phil even took a shot at our car as we drove away.

What can we do?

Signed,

At Least The Squatters Seem To Like Us

Dear At Least,

Your problem is a common one, and it is a matter of managing expectations. Each family unit believes that it should be the focal point in your lives, and so competes for your time and attention. You should take this as a sign that they all love you and just crave your company.

My suggestion would be to fake your own deaths and move to Tahiti.

Dear Dr. Funny Guy,

I'm getting pretty sick of all the seasonal jokes about fruitcakes. This is a serious problem! Our regular postal carrier was injured just before Christmas when he had to hit the brakes of his mail truck and the fruitcakes stacked up behind him shifted forward. It took a backhoe and the Jaws of Life nearly two days to dig him out.

So what are we supposed to do with all these fruitcakes we receive every year? I'm afraid that if we throw them away, they could reach critical mass in the landfills, fall to the center of the planet, and create a black hole that will destroy our entire section of the galaxy.

I heard that Lou Dobbs has proposed a Fruit Cake Plan - something about Mexicans. Could there be any truth to this?

Signed,

Stephen Hawking

Dear Dr. Hawking,

While the research certainly does support your fruitcake black hole theory, I don't think we have much to worry about. For one thing, if that many people threw away their fruitcakes, the axles on all the garbage trucks would break long before they got to the landfill.

I agree with you though, fruitcakes are a serious problem in our society. While a few of them have been successfully used as ballast in Liberian freighters, there are just not enough freighters out there to provide a permanent solution.

I recently encountered several people who claim to like fruitcakes, and who actually eat them. My thought is that if we can identify these people, we could send all the fruitcakes to them.

The only downside I can see is that concentrating all the fruitcakes in these few locations might upset the orbit of the planet and plunge us into the sun. Still, it would probably be worth it.

As for the Lou Dobbs thing, that was just an unfounded rumor started by an unscrupulous humor columnist. I'm sure that even Mr. Dobbs would never inflict fruitcakes on Mexicans.

If you have critical life issues to deal with, and you would like advice from a professional village idiot, send your questions to:

DrMike@LearnedSoFar.com.

Election Night 2008

He might be somewhere in the neighborhood of eighty years old. He is tall and lean and weathered and black, and he looks like he is right at home under the Virginia sun. He has been standing in line for two hours, with his equally weathered wife at his side, and he is still less than half way through the line. He is calmly and happily waiting for his turn to vote.

The television reporter asks him how he feels, and a shy smile lights up his face as he opens his mouth to speak. But then his voice catches in his throat, and he has to cough and clear his throat and wipe the corner of his eye before he can answer. He looks at his wife, and says, "I never thought I'd see this day."

I'm walking to work and a conservatively dressed white man in his sixties stops me to

hand me a "Don't Forget To Vote" door hanger.
His haircut, polished shoes and wool jacket say
"lawyer," or maybe "accountant." The logo on the
door hanger he gives me says, "Barack Obama."

The 125,000 people in Chicago's Grant Park
are cheering and chanting and celebrating the
announcement that the election has been called in
favor of Obama. Among all those radiant faces -
mostly young, all ecstatic - a balding man, about
my age, stands out because he is not smiling, or
screaming, or jumping up and down. He is staring
ahead in disbelief. Tears run down his cheeks. He
is simply overwhelmed.

Something important has happened.

I've been around for quite a few years. I
listened to Dr. King tell us about his dream, and
I wept when the forces of hatred and intolerance
took him away from us. I listened to Bobby
Kennedy plead for peace in the face of that
overwhelming pain, and I wept again when those
same dark forces took him.

I lived through LBJ, and hippies, and
Vietnam, and Watergate, and race riots, and gas
lines, and Reaganomics. I've spent my entire
adult life in a country divided along cultural and
ideological and racial lines. As America's problems
became more difficult over the past few years, I
watched those lines deepen and harden, and I

listened as political rhetoric seemed every day to turn more poisonous and hateful.

At first, this election campaign seemed to develop along those same lines. We saw grainy pictures of Barack Obama in a turban, and listened to robocalls that told us that he was a socialist and a terrorist. We heard people at rallies, whipped to a frenzy by the candidates, shout "Kill Him!" and "Terrorist!" and "Off With His Head!"

But then something happened. This time the American people rejected the divisiveness that served recent political campaigns so effectively. This time the people refused to retreat to fear and slogans. They rejected the dark suggestions that Barack Obama was somehow "other" and "dangerous." Every time the McCain campaign turned up the negative volume – to the apparent discomfort of John McCain, a man I have deeply admired for many years - the polls stayed the same or moved in Obama's favor.

And tonight, by an overwhelming margin, the people elected Barack Obama President of the United States of America.

I can't say that President Obama will have the answers to all our problems, or even most of them. I do know that he has the intellectual capacity to explore and grasp them, the willingness to build teams to attack them, and the personal magnetism to inspire those teams to success.

Tonight Barack Obama gave his victory speech on a stage in Grant Park, ironically the same place where I first found out about tear gas during the 1968 Democratic National Convention. And as I listened to him I had to think that maybe we are seeing the end of the culture wars we have endured for so many years. He began by saying, "If there is anyone out there who doubts that America is a place where all things are possible…"

Something important happened tonight.

2009 – The Year in Preview

So now the champagne bottles are in the recycling bin, most of the confetti is in the trash bag, and we have bid a fond farewell to the year gone by as it swirled festively down the old toilet. That means that it's time once again for my annual Year In Preview edition.

I almost didn't write this one. Not too long ago, I heard from a helpful reader who pointed out that in all my previous Preview columns I had failed to get so much as one thing completely right. He went on to compare me to the Republican party who, according to him, have not managed to get anything right since the Eisenhower administration. I think that's a little unfair. I was only nine when Eisenhower left office.

But anyway, here goes:

January, 2009 - President Barack Obama is inaugurated the 44th President of the United States. The ceremony has to be briefly interrupted so that Secret Service agents can rescue former President George W. Bush, who wandered off during the invocation and got his tongue stuck to a flagpole.

Obama's first executive order is to assign a Special Ops team to locate the lair of former Vice President Dick Cheney and extract him from the White House.

February, 2009 - A valentine card from Bill O'Reilly, addressed to Anne Coulter, is discovered in the No Spin Zone. When it is opened, a computer chip in the card plays My Funny Valentine, while flaming streams of pure evil shoot out and consume the Fox News studio.

April, 2009 - To aid in the nation's economic recovery, the IRS decides to accept "World of WarCraft" gold for tax payments. This brings untold joy to Herb Saltzman, a Level 80 Orc Warrior who lives in his mom's basement in Newark, New Jersey, and it completely baffles pretty much everybody else.

June, 2009 - Paris Hilton reads in People magazine that the Rottweiler is the new Designer Dog. She immediately buys one, names it

"Tinkerbelle Zwei" and is critically mauled when she tries to stuff it into a Louis Vuitton handbag.

July, 2009 - CNN is criticized for being racially insensitive when it airs footage of the Obama family eating watermelon at a Fourth of July picnic. Asked for comment, President Obama says, "Geeze, get over it. I happen to like watermelon." Later, the President is overheard telling an aide, "Man, it's a good thing they didn't see my six-pack of Colt 45!"

September, 2009 - Nintendo releases a new game for the Wii system called "Symphonic Orchestra Hero." You and up to 100 of your friends stand in for members of the New York Philharmonic, "playing" instruments like plastic Stradivarius violins.

On a related note, a substantial portion of downtown Vienna, Austria sustained damage from earth tremors caused by Mozart spinning in his grave.

November, 2009 - Illinois Governor Rod Blagojevich is convicted on 259 counts of corruption and sentenced to 40 years in federal prison. In a post-sentencing statement to reporters outside the courtroom he winks, gives a "thumbs-up" and says, "Well, I'm very, very pleased to be cleared of any legal wrongdoing, any hint of any kind of unethical activity there. Very pleased to be cleared of any of that."

Blagojevich is immediately sued for plagiarism by Alaska Governor Sarah Palin.

December, 2009 - The holiday season is nearly ruined when an F/A-18 on a routine patrol flight in the Persian Gulf accidentally fires an AIM missile at Santa Claus. Santa rolls out into a 6-G turn, deploys a chaff anti-radar countermeasure (tosses a bag of tinsel out of the sleigh), and is able to evade the missile.

The F/A-18 pilot is reprimanded by the Navy, and is put on Santa's "Really Naughty" list.

Well that's it for another year. Remember, if any of this stuff happens it will all be news to me.

Dark Winter Days

January in Michigan means the sharp smell of wood smoke in the crisp winter air, the windblown drifts of purest snow outlining the soft contours of the compost heap, the thrill of skidding on one heel across an icy parking lot with an armload of groceries, and the chore of chipping snotcicles from the tip of your frostbitten nose.

But as wonderful as this season may be in so many ways, some of us are not all that crazy about the fact that we get to see the sun for maybe an hour a month. Not only are the days ridiculously short, but we also have a shroud of clouds parked overhead pretty much from November through March.

The Gray Days are so profound around here that they can cause their very own form of clinical depression, a psychological disorder with maybe the most appropriate acronym ever – SAD. This stands for Seasonal Affective Disorder, and it pretty much boils down to sufferers being clinically pissed off about all the crappy weather.

SAD is really common in places like Scandinavia, spreading deep and persistent despair up there where they have even shorter, grayer days than we have, and nothing but Volvos to drive.

You can treat SAD by sitting in front of a bright white therapeutic light for half an hour, once or twice a day. If that's not enough to cheer you up, I sure don't know what would be.

Last weekend we had a freakish lack of clouds here for a few hours, so I went for a walk to soak up a little bit of sun, and to visit some Austrian friends who were holding an "Austrian Curling" tournament on the lake.

In the version of Curling we usually see on TV (when we can't find any Star Trek reruns to watch), one player slides a big "stone" down the ice at a bunch of other stones. The part I like best is when two teammates carrying brooms run along with the stone, scrubbing the ice like crazy, and shouting gibberish back and forth with a guy at the other end of the ice.

I kind of thought Austrian curling would be just like that, except maybe instead of sliding stones down the ice, we would be sliding the

Austrians. It turns out that there were no sliding Austrians, at least not intentionally, and for that matter no brooms. But the sport did involve some shouted gibberish and a fair amount of hot spiced wine, so we all had a real good time.

It's funny how much it can boost your spirits to see a little sunshine. As we all stood chatting on the lake, drinking our hot spiced wine and watching the moisture in our breath freeze in midair and clatter to the ice, we kept remarking on what a beautiful day it was. Of course, maybe the friends had at least as much to do with the beauty of the day as the quality of the light.

Now that I think of it, I can remember many years ago, sliding down Kid-crusher Hill on a toboggan, hanging with a death grip onto whoever was in front of me and squeezed almost breathless by whoever was behind me, all of us woven into a stocking-capped chain of friends. I can remember the end of each run, our chain collapsed into a body pile of snow-crusted kids, all of us laughing so hard we were choking, smelling like wet wool mittens and Juicy Fruit gum.

I can remember skating on a frozen tennis court that some nameless benefactor had flooded for our benefit, cheeks burning with exertion, swatting the one hockey puck we had with our pine hockey sticks, and digging frantically in the snow pile for it whenever one of our slap shots came up a little frisky.

I can remember being in snowball fights that tactically duplicated major Napoleonic artillery battles, finding refuge from the bombardment behind the snowman we were so careful to protect just a couple of hours before, while we were making him.

What I don't remember about any of those days is whether the sun was shining. Knowing the odds, probably not. I guess back then if we needed therapeutic lights we could always find one lying in the snow right next to us.

Making snow angels.

Ryan's Song

His name was Ryan, and he was not the most popular guy in the group. He was a big country boy with big farmer arms and a big farmer face, the kind of kid some people might call a "bumpkin." On this particular day he was outnumbered nine to one by street smart city kids.

We were sitting in a circle on a dimly lit stage in the maximum-security WJ Maxey Boys Training School for incarcerated young men, working on a collaborative song about a guy who is, coincidentally, being released after serving time in a maximum-security facility.

This was one of the first Lost Voices sessions ever, and Josh White, Jr. and I were figuring out how we might translate the thoughts and poetry of these troubled kids into original folk and blues music. The process was working well, but it was intense almost beyond belief.

We were taking a break to catch our breath when Ryan spoke up, "I wrote a poem in my room last night. It's about this one time when my uncle took me fishing. Do you want to hear it?" We did. He began to read.

It's early morning, down at the lake
Me and my fishing gear
All of my worries, and all of my cares
Just seem to disappear.
Talking 'bout a young boy's dream
Walking by the side of a stream
Thinking about the good times
That's good fishing, all the time.

As Ryan read, I could hear those words bouncing along in a happy John Denver kind of song. Key of D for sure. I started playing it and a smile lit up Ryan's face. Josh joined in with harmony when we got to the chorus, and Ryan's grin went nuclear.

At the end of the program there was a concert, in which the boys went on stage with us to perform the songs we had written. As the concert approached, Josh and I asked Ryan if he wanted us to sing his song for him, or if he was willing to sing it himself. We like to challenge the kids, but we try to be careful not to push them into doing anything they are not comfortable with. "I want to sing it myself," he said, "Maybe with a little help from you and Josh!"

And then came the moment in the concert when I introduced Ryan and invited him up to the microphone. There was a good-sized audience, several hundred people. Virtually every kid in the facility was there, plus most of the teachers, the staff, and a bunch of VIP strangers. The spotlights were just bright enough to make us want to squint, but not bright enough to hide all those people.

Ryan's face was frozen in a mask of dread as he stepped forward and I strummed the pick-up chords. I learned several weeks after the fact that in that moment he was dealing with a lot more than simple performance jitters; it seems that a number of the guys who did not care too much for country boys, especially bumpkins named "Ryan," had promised to "tear him up" if he tried to perform.

But still Ryan stepped forward.

When he started to sing, fear had such a stranglehold on his throat that the words were just barely able to squeeze past vocal chords stretched tight with terror.

But still Ryan started to sing.

When we got to the chorus, the audience began to clap along - a few of them at first, then more, and finally the whole room, clapping and stomping in time. Ryan's paralysis dissolved, and his voice got stronger as he sang verse after verse about that magic morning when he went down to the lake and caught himself a Smallmouth bass.

And then we found ourselves at the end of the song. Ryan stood in the center of the stage grinning that big old country boy grin as the audience - including the anti-bumpkin contingent - gave him and his song a standing ovation.

Talk about a young boy's dream.

Not All Pirates Carry Guns

OK, something has been bothering me. Exactly how can a handful of pirates in a small boat take over a 17,000 ton cargo ship?

I just read about the daring rescue of Captain Richard Phillips, the incredibly heroic freighter captain who gave himself up as a hostage to Somali pirates to keep them from harming his crew. He spent five days in a lifeboat with his captors, until some snipers on an American warship gave a pretty convincing demonstration of the basic drawbacks you might face if you happen to take up a career in pirating.

But what I don't understand is how the pirates keep getting on board in the first place. Have you ever been near one of those ships? They're huge! It's not like you can just pull up alongside, knock on the door, and say, "Good afternoon, sir. Somali pirates here, and we've come around to take you hostage. Mind if we come in?"

Apparently what these guys do is climb ropes up the side of the ship, slinging their assault rifles behind them, and (presumably) clenching cutlasses between their teeth. So to become a pirate, you apparently have to have successfully passed the fitness test in Mr. Frick's 7th grade gym class. With an AK-47.

But this raises the question of how those ropes got there in the first place. If freighters are sailing around the seas near Somalia trailing nice fat ropes, with knots tied at the bottom to make for easy climbing, then I believe we may have just discovered one way to seriously curtail Somali piracy.

Of course, I have a feeling that it may not be quite that simple. Maybe the pirates come alongside and throw grappling hooks over the railing, or shoot the ropes up there with launchers, just like action movie cat burglars and Batman.

In that case, though, it seems like the crew of the freighter would notice all that hook-throwing and rope shooting, wander over, and as the incoming pirates pop up, and simply bash them on the head with a bottle of grog, or some other handy bit of nautical equipment. Kind of like a seafaring game of Whack-A-Mole.

I'm clearly missing something here.

You know, I have pretty much the same question about the pirates who somehow got aboard the largest financial institutions in the world and have spent the last few years looting the global economy. How did we not notice all those guys scaling the side of the J.P. Morgan Building?

Maybe it's because they wear Armani suits instead of grubby shorts and dirty tank tops. They show up in limos or executive helicopters, rather than little boats with big engines. And when they lose a major battle, they just have to fire a few servants and maybe sell off one of the mansions in The Hamptons.

I think a big reason we never paid much attention to the Wall Street buccaneers is that they don't carry their weapons in plain view. They overpower us using things called "derivatives," which have pretty much the same destructive power as an assault rifle, but they're not nearly as noisy.

Or maybe we looked the other way because we felt like they were letting us in on some of the action. Piracy just doesn't seem to be quite as vile when it's returning eight percent, net, as part of a mutual fund in your 401K portfolio.

So the pirates from Somalia have extorted millions of dollars from the shipping companies.

The ones from Wall Street have pocketed billions from peoples' life savings and pension funds. Maybe tens of billions. Hundreds of billions? Trillions? Nobody is quite sure.

But one thing you can be sure of is that not many of those Wall Street pirates are going to wind up like the Somalis who were holding Captain Phillips, with a bullet between the eyes inscribed "Property Of The United States Navy."

In a way, that seems like a pity, doesn't it?

Modern Communication

I just read about a couple in India who got married by cell phone, because the groom got caught in a monsoon and couldn't make it through the flood waters to get to the wedding.

Wow! Talk about blowing away that last really great excuse! After this, those of you who thought you were going to fall back on the old "Honey, I tried to make it home in time to go to the third grade clarinet recital, but a monsoon washed the road out!" story will have to come up with something new.

I wonder how fifteen out-of-tune clarinets would sound over a cell phone?

Admittedly, that little lump of technology in your pocket or purse can keep you within striking range of just about every variety of nagging and harassment. But try not to get too down on the little guy – it also opens up a whole world of possibilities. For one thing, your cell phone is an invaluable safety tool. It lets you immediately call for help if you've broken down on the highway, or for your spouse if you become separated in the Discount Club store.

And then there is my friend who uses his cell phone and a sound effects tape in his car to orchestrate excuses for every occasion. Through the magic of electronics, he can sit in the lot at the golf course and call his boss from a traffic jam, the emergency room, an airport ticket counter, or the examination room of a spaceship bound for the Crab Nebula; "They're probing me – noooooooooo!"

If you do this though, be very careful not to record your sounds over a used tape. My friend had a hard time explaining to his wife why Gwen Stefani suddenly started singing during the "prayer service" that was going on in his Buick parked outside the tavern.

Of course, there will be times when you don't want to be at the mercy of your cell phone. For those of you who would like to learn to live with or even get the upper hand on your little electronic pal, there are a lot of things you can do that are a little more creative than turning the thing off and not knowing how to retrieve your voice mail.

First, there's the "Gosh, I must have dropped the cell or something!" gambit. This one is best used on people who just haven't figured out that the conversation pretty much ended about ten minutes ago. The key to success here is to start a sentence; "Oh, I almost forgot to tell you about the grzzzzznxxxxt..." And then turn off the power.

Of course there are almost endless variations you can use. The real secret is to master an assortment of "static" noises.

Then there's the "I'll have to call you back – I'm getting into heavy traffic – AAAAAaaaarghhhhh!" routine. This one is good when you just didn't look closely enough at the caller ID before you answered the call. Later, you can tell your caller all about the near miss you had while you were talking to them.

Come to think of it, wouldn't a "near miss" essentially be a "hit?"

Finally, there's the "I have to hang up now because I've reached the front of the line at the bank, and the cashier just handed me a threatening note!" ploy.

Hey! How about just hanging up before you go into the bank?

Nah.

After the Super Bowl

Well, it's over. The Pittsburgh Steelers are dumping champagne over each others' Super Bowl XLIII Champion caps and thanking their Lord and Savior for standing by them and guiding every savage hit on an opponent from the very beginning of this long, tough NFL season. Meanwhile, the Arizona Cardinals are quietly waxing philosophical and consoling each other with a cold beer – probably not Steel City.

So what have we really accomplished here today?

For one thing, as a game-watching nation we wolfed down something like 1.2 billion chicken wings and 15 thousand tons of chips, along with enough ranch dressing, salsa, onion dip and guacamole to turn the Grand Canyon into a scenic condiment bowl. Some statistician with a lot of time on his hands has actually calculated that the amount of Orville Redenbacher we chowed would make a popcorn string long enough to stretch more than 5.5 laps around the world.

And we washed it all down with 52 million cases of beer.

The Super Bowl is also the number one day on the American calendar for blowing money on stupid bets. We plop down an estimated 8 billion dollars on every kind of wager that devious minds can dream up, including exactly how long the National Anthem will take and how many times in each sentence John Madden will make a food reference (the current over/under on that last one is 1.5). Vegas was even giving four-to-one pre-game odds against Bruce Springsteen opening his halftime show by singing "The Rising."

And then, of course, there are the commercials. On the day after every year's Super Bowl, at least among the gridiron luddites I hang around with, the water cooler rehash is not even remotely about the game. It is about Conan O'Brian crawling across a foam-lathered stage in a red mesh tank top, crooning an ad slogan in Swedish.

What we have here is American companies thumbing their corporate noses at the tough economic climate and spending upwards of 3 million dollars for each of sixty-nine thirty second ad slots. Instead of throwing in the towel, they will invest more than 206 million dollars in themselves and in selling their products.

With that kind of money on the line, they naturally try to put the most creative work they can come up with into those little solid platinum time slots. This year, in addition to Conan, we have had a Clydesdale who knew how to fetch, a box of flowers telling the recipient that nobody wants to see her naked, and a pretty fair-sized chunk of the insect kingdom banding together to steal a guy's Coke.

It just doesn't get any better than that.

From a sport purist's point of view, this year's Super Bowl was a much better football game than a lot of them have been. Sometimes in the past we've spent our five hours watching the gang of sportscasters and ex-jocks on the air struggling to make a pathetic blowout sound like the contest of the millennium.

And since the vast majority of Super Bowl viewers live outside the market areas of the two teams who are playing, even that good old chest-painting, shaving the quarterback's number in your hair, drunk since 8 am in the parking lot brand of fan loyalty is not really that much of a factor. There is only enough of all that on hand to spice up the pre-game show.

So the Super Bowl is always more about the party than about the game. A bunch of millionaire athletes get enormous cash bonuses, and we get to spend the next two weeks on the Stairmaster trying to work off all that beer and queso. But everybody involved has some real fun in the process.

Sort of makes you proud to be an American, doesn't it?

Caveat eMptor

I've discovered something at least as addictive as caffeine, alcohol, tobacco, cocaine, heroin, or even Chex Mix (the really good homemade kind, with way too much garlic salt). At this moment millions of people around the world are sitting, huddled, alone, sweating, shaking, counting down the seconds until they can "get right" with their next "fix."

I'm talking, of course, about eBay, the Internet equivalent of the bazaar at Marrakech. This is the well-known online auction service where you can buy anything from clothespins to cattle prods, often paying less than 70 times the actual value of the item.

eBay was founded in 1995 by Pierre Omidyar, a computer programmer who allegedly wanted to help his fiancée buy and sell PEZ candy dispensers. The first item actually sold on eBay was a broken laser pointer, purchased for $14.83 (plus shipping) by a guy who, it turns out, is a noted collector of broken laser pointers.

On this rock solid intellectual foundation, a cultural icon for the twenty-first century was born.

I recently decided to take my first dip in the eBay pool when I needed a microphone, and I just did not want to mess around with all the messy warranties and buyer's confidence that go along with buying a new one. So I went to eBay and did a search on the word "Microphone."

The first listing that popped up looked interesting. There was a photograph, a little out of focus, of an object that appeared to be exactly the kind of microphone I was looking for. Next to the picture was a compelling item title:

mik - lik nu bargin!!!!! Bids: 15 Price: $27.50
Time Left: 18 m

Wow! A lik nu bargin!!!!! And with less than twenty minutes left in the auction, the price was only up to $27.50! With trembling fingers I clicked for more information. I was greeted with a larger out-of-focus photograph of the microphone-like object and a detailed technical description of the equipment:

> *it kind look like real gud mikrofon so probly is.*
> *shiping to usa $45*

After several minutes of forehead-wrinkling thought I decided that the shipping charges looked a little steep on this otherwise fantastic bargain.

In less than nine hours I had worked my way almost a quarter of the way through all the microphones for sale on eBay. With a little experimentation I learned that I could narrow down my quest by changing the search to "Microphone – Not A Transparent Scam," which took the number of items found from 12,452 to 11.

I finally picked out what looked like the perfect microphone for me. It was time to take my first shot at making a purchase, so with trembling fingers I entered an amount two dollars above the "current bid."

The screen immediately flashed, a loud "BOOP" sounded, and huge red letters appeared shouting, "YOU'VE BEEN OUTBID!" It turns out that eBay has an automatic bidding system, where you can enter the highest amount you're willing to pay for something and the computer will automatically outbid newcomers by a dollar or two, until either the auction passes your maximum bid or the time runs out.

So I entered what I thought the microphone was worth, including the ten dollar "shipping and handling" fee, and sat back to watch the fun. Then, as the last few minutes ticked down and with my bid still in the lead, I felt the adrenaline start to take over.

With two minutes to go, a cascade of bids passed mine. Only my fumble-fingered keyboard technique kept me from jumping back into the fray to buy that used microphone for a final price that was about three dollars more than it would have cost new in the box at the music store.

Over the next week I repeated this ritual a few times until I developed my own never-fail bidding method. All I do is enter my maximum bid, then have my wife lock me in the linen closet until it's all over. Using this technique I eventually did get my used microphone, and at a great price. Now I need a cord to attach it to the amplifier:

eBay Search: "Microphone Cables – Probably Not Blatant Rip-off."

Spring Ski Trip, Part 1:
Half the Fun is Getting There

"To-ho-hod Ju-hu-hun-ior, pl-he-he-ase st-ho-hop th-ha-ha-hat!"

Todd Junior, who has been rhythmically testing the soles of his new snowboard boots on the back of Dad's car seat for the past three hundred miles, thumps his feet down to the floor mat and punches Little Suzy in the arm.

Little Suzie clicks the "pause" button on her iPod, yawns, stretches, then shoves Bernie the Schnauzer, who has been sleeping in the rear window shelf behind Todd Junior's head, onto Todd Junior's head.

Two hours later, once Mom has mopped all the Schnauzer pee out of Todd Junior's hair and

the AAA wrecker has pulled the family sedan out
of the snow bank, the family is on the road again.

This year, instead of the annual Florida
trip, they are headed to Mount Feverblister, for
what the Ski Resort brochure describes as "The
Feverblister Winter Sports Paradise Package and
All-You-Can-Eat Buffet." There they will meet up
with Aunt Meg, Uncle Bob, the Twins (Bobby
and Robby), and Little Pammie, who have been
enjoying ski vacations at Mount Feverblister
for years.

Mom, Dad, Todd Junior and Little Suzy have
never been skiing before, so an hour before dawn
that morning they pulled away from home with
$7, 265 worth of brand new ski and snowboard
equipment strapped to the roof of the sedan.
Hours later, when they stopped for lunch, Dad
discovered that the big "pop" he heard on that
long bridge a hundred miles back was the ski rack
breaking loose and sailing into the river.

Just after dark, the family sedan pulls into
the Mount Feverblister Ski Resort, which is also
known as the East Possum Bladder Best Western.
While Dad checks in and gets the room keys,
Mom stands in the parking lot comparing the Ski
Resort brochure with the scenery in the area, and
for the first time truly appreciates the marketing
power of stock photography.

Once Dad has carried everything that had not been strapped to the roof rack up to the room, everybody washes up and puts on fresh clothes. Then Dad hustles his hungry family down for the nightly All-You-Can-Eat Buffet Dinner that is included in their Paradise Package.

The only people in the dining room are Aunt Meg, Uncle Bob, and the kids, sitting at a large table. They each have a plate in front of them heaped with breaded chicken wings, macaroni with cheese, and orange Jell-O.

"Hey there, ski bums," shouts Uncle Bob. "Grab a plate and join us – we saved you a seat!"

The buffet, in addition to the breaded chicken wings, macaroni with cheese, and orange Jell-O, contains a pan of something resembling rice, and a greenish substance that may have once been broccoli, or possibly okra. Everyone sticks with the breaded chicken wings, macaroni with cheese, and orange Jell-O.

After they've finished eating, Todd Junior and the Twins trade under-the-table shin kicks from their snowboarding boots. Little Suzie and Pammie compare and contrast the contents of their iPods. Mom and Aunt Meg debate how you could have fish bones in breaded chicken wings. Dad fills Uncle Bob in on the details of the trip,

and explains how they seem to have lost all
their equipment.

Uncle Bob assures Dad that they can rent
all the ski or snowboarding gear they'll need
tomorrow morning at the Mountain. When Mom
asks Uncle Bob where that alleged Mountain
might be, Uncle Bob laughs and explains that
Mount Feverblister is actually a giant sanitary
landfill about a quarter of a mile up the road from
the Best Western.

"The beauty of the whole thing," says Uncle
Bob," is that you not only get to ski down the hill
they made covering up all that garbage, why then
you just zip right on down into the hole they dug
doing it!"

An hour later, since the television in the
room is broken and there is not a single bar
open anywhere near East Possum Bladder, the
whole family is settled down in bed, there to
rest up and dream of tomorrow and the big ski
adventure to come.

Next week: Sliding Down the Garbage.

Spring Ski Trip, Part 2: Sliding Down the Garbage

"Four lift tickets - two adult, two children. That will be $312.50."

"You don't understand," Dad explains patiently. "We're here on the Mount Feverblister Winter Sports Paradise Package and All-You-Can-Eat Buffet. It says right there in the brochure, 'Lift Tickets Included.'"

The woman in the ticket booth puts down her Danielle Steel paperback and scans Dad's brochure. "What's included is Tickets to catch a Lift on the Mogul-Buster Express from the resort to the hill. See the footnote right there?"

"The Mogul-Buster Express? Are you talking about that panel van with four flat tires in the parking lot at the East Possum Bladder Best Western? The one with the 'Mogul-Buster Express' signs taped over the rust holes?"

"That's the one. Good thing you didn't have a lot of stuff to carry on the walk over here. Which reminds me, the Ski Rental is right over there. $312.50 please."

*****

The Mount Feverblister Ski Rental is a cinder block building with a concrete floor. Pine boards laid across stacks of cinder blocks form rows of shelves that hold bright green ski boots, hand-numbered with hot pink glitter paint. An apparently random assortment of skis, poles and snowboards, all prominently numbered with the same hot pink paint, lean around the walls. The air is heavy with the smell of ozone and 3-In-One oil.

The attendant is wearing a white-ish turtleneck sweater, white-ish nylon pants, and wrap-around sunglasses in a windowless building lit by a single 100 watt bulb. A large plastic badge pinned to his sweater says, "Master Ski Technician," with the name "Chad" written below (in hot pink glitter paint).

"So," says Chad, "would you like me to set you up with high-performance racing, or recreational equipment?

"I want a 'Hill Crusher Supreme' snowboard," shrieks Todd Junior.

"We're all just learning, so we'd like something easy to use," says Mom.

"I think I'd like to try out a downhill racing ski," says Dad. "Maybe something with titanium alloy-reinforced torsion box construction and triaxial braiding. Oh, and racing boots, please."

"I'm going to walk back to the hotel," says little Suzie.

*****

Standing at last at the summit of Mount Feverblister, Dad takes a deep breath and says, "Just smell that mountain air!"

"It's a sanitary landfill," says Mom. "I think that might be cabbage."

"Dad, why is your left ski a different brand from the right one?" asks Todd Junior.

"If you had been listening when Chad explained it, you would know that it's to give me maximum performance for high-speed racing turns. This ski is optimized to my right, or 'dominant' leg, while this one is optimized to my left."

"It's definitely not because there were only two skis with functional bindings that would work on the only pair of boots that would fit him," says Mom.

"Hey, Chad is a Master Ski Technician," says Dad. "He told me this is how all the best Olympic skiers do it."

Uncle Bob hops off the chair lift and skids to a stop in front of Dad. "Hey, there you ski bums are. We've been here for hours… whoa, those are some interesting skis."

"Yeah, Chad figures that I'm athlete enough to handle them."

"Right. Well, last one down's a rotten head of cabbage," says Uncle Bob as he launches himself down the hill.

"Shouldn't we start on the 'Bunny Hill?'" asks Mom.

"'Bunny Hill!' We don't need no stinkin' 'Bunny Hill,'" says Dad in his best Treasure of Sierra Madre Mexican bandito accent.

Dad poles himself over to the edge of the hill. "All right guys, here we g…AAAAAAAAAAAAAA AAAAAAAAAAAAAAAAAAAAAAAAAAAAA!"

Next week: A Visit To The East Possum Bladder Urgent Care.

Spring Ski Trip, Part 3:
A Visit to the East Possum
Bladder Urgent Care

"How many fingers am I holding up?" asks the young woman in the maroon Mount Feverblister Ski Patrol jacket.

"Just one," says Dad, "and I kind of wish you wouldn't use that particular finger, turned around like that."

"Okay, Chad, he's alert," says the young woman. "Let's get him strapped to the back board."

"I'm not sure 'alert' would be the word I would choose," says a young man, presumably Chad, also wearing a maroon Mount Feverblister Ski Patrol jacket and peering over the young woman's shoulder. "An 'alert,' person wouldn't have taken out that whole beginner's class of hearing-impaired kids when he shot across the Bunny Hill."

"I yelled, 'Look Out!'" says Dad.

"Just after you crashed through that great big warning sign that said 'Caution – Hearing-Impaired Kids.'"

"You know, you'd think that a sign like that would have slowed me down more than it did."

"Yes, you would," says the young woman. "Or hitting all those tables in the outdoor café. Or crashing through the gift shop."

"Who'd guess they made those walls that thin. So, apparently it was the front of that Prius that launched me airborne in the parking lot."

"Apparently," says the young woman. "I kind of liked the way you sort of banked off the dumpster lid and into the dumpster."

"Probably saved my life."

*****

"He has a few scrapes and bruises, and a slight sprain in his left ankle. All in all, I'd say he's pretty lucky," says the bearded man with the stethoscope draped across the collar of his green flannel shirt and the name badge reading, "Dr. Chad" in hot pink glitter paint. "He'll be out in a couple of minutes."

"Thank you, Doctor," says Mom. "Todd Junior, please put those down."

"Awwww," says Todd Junior as he (temporarily) drops the defibrillator paddles he was holding to his cousin Pammie's ears while the Twins looked for the "on" switch.

"Thank goodness Dad is all right," says Little Suzie, surreptitiously pocketing rolls of surgical tape and gauze for something she has planned for later that night; a little game she likes to call "When Todd Junior Wakes Up He'll Discover That He's a Mummy."

"You're certainly right," says Aunt Meg, surreptitiously pocketing sample bottles of Demerol and OxyContin for something she has planned for later that night; a little game she likes to call "Taking Aunt Meg To Her Happy Place."

"Oh, and another thing," says Dr. Chad over his shoulder as he heads for the Doctor's Lounge, "make sure he doesn't try to go skiing again."

"Until his ankle has had a chance to heal?" asks Mom.

"Ever."

At that moment Uncle Bob pushes Dad out of the examining room in a wheelchair. "Good as new," he says. "And we're just in time to get back for the All You Can Eat Buffet! This is the night they sprinkle Bacon Bits on the macaroni with cheese!"

"My favorite," says Aunt Meg.

"Sounds great," says Mom.

"Yippee," says Dad.

"Why isn't there a Taco Bell in this county?" says Little Suzie.

"Clear!" shouts Todd Junior.

And the lights go out all over metropolitan East Possum Bladder.

Author's Note: This has been a work of fiction. Any resemblance of the characters depicted here to actual persons, living, deceased, or in traction, is purely coincidental. But it does sound kind of familiar, doesn't it?

Champions

As I am writing this, the Detroit Red Wings have just won their third playoff finals game against the Pittsburgh Penguins and are one victory away from winning the 2008 Stanley Cup. If they win, we here in Michigan intend to annex South Dakota so we can put Pavel Datsyuk, Henrik Zetterberg, Tomas Holmstrom and coach Mike Babcock (a Russian, two Swedes and a Canadian) on Mount Rushmore.

At the same time, the Detroit Pistons players are all dusting off their golf clubs after being knocked out of the conference championship by the Boston Celtics. A lot of Detroit fans are calling sports talk shows to debate whether Pistons coach Flip Saunders should be fired, shot, poisoned, burned at the stake, fed to hungry alligators, or given a public relations job in the Bush Administration.

And the Detroit Tigers are… well, they're the Tigers.

As you're reading this, you probably know quite a bit more than I do about how all that stuff is working out. But I can't help wondering why we sports fans even care. After all, whether Darren McCarty gets to float around in a swimming pool sipping Crown Royal and Red Pop out of the Stanley Cup or not, my life will be pretty much the same.

And boy, do we fans ever care! We drive around with team flags flapping themselves into colorful shreds by our car windows. We sit for hours in front of the television set, screaming helpful coaching tips at the screen. We paint our cars, our boats, and even our homes in team colors. We name our pet hamsters after the team's equipment manager.

Well, some of us do.

In return for all this unbridled adulation, we expect championships. If our team doesn't happen to win it all, we pull for them to come close enough that we can accuse all the other teams of shameless cheating and assure each other that we'll get 'em next year.

Just what is it that gives us the right to demand so much of our teams? On the surface, I think it's all about wanting some return for our commitment. After all, if I'm going to spend eight bucks on an adjustable billed cap with a team's logo on it, I have a right to expect every member of that team's organization to lay down his or her life to live up to my idea of success.

But it may be a lot more than that. I think that at some level we each imagine ourselves to be the one on the ice firing a slap shot at the net, or driving the lane for a lay-up, or getting hit in the butt with a knuckle ball.

That being the case, it seems like people who have participated in one sport or another, especially those of us who have been fortunate enough to have been involved with winning any sort of championship, would have a more realistic attitude when we toss our athletic supporters in the laundry and sit down to become fans. We all know from experience that no matter who or how good you are, for every time you hoist a trophy, there had to be a lot more times when you shake the winner's hand and hoist a conciliatory beer.

As I write this I don't know for sure how the Stanley Cup Finals will turn out. At the moment the Red Wings' odds look pretty good, and within the next few days there's a pretty good chance that I'll get to see my boys skating around with the Cup held over their heads. At the same time, I try to remember that in every contest there is one team that gets called "champion," and all the other teams have to wait until next year.

But you know what? This year, it really better be my Red Wings. After all, I did buy a cap…

Oh, My Aching Back

My back hurts.

It's not the first time. Over the years I've performed unplanned high speed front flips into the water while I was riding the Air Chair behind the ski boat. I've thrown my body at linebackers the size of an SUV - a real SUV, not one of those silly little Japanese jobbies that probably wouldn't make it across the Baja hauling more than about 250 grocery bags full of Wonder Bread and Spaghetti-Os. I've gripped my hockey stick with cheerful determination and skated headfirst into opposing players who were bigger, stronger, and more talented than I was - and who saw me coming.

My Physical Therapist has a coffee cup in the waiting room with my name on it.

So yes, I'm fairly familiar with the whole concept of screwing myself up. The difference is that this time I can't explain my debilitating injury with a hearty tale of courage, daring, and sheer stupidity. This time my back pain is not some sort of karmic pay-back for an idea that was almost as much fun as it was ill-advised. This time what happened was, I bent over to pick up a piece of paper.

That's right. Six years ago I won a national championship for water skiing while balancing a girl over my head on one hand. Now I've missed work and become best friends with the chiropractor over one ill-advised clean and jerk on a gum wrapper. I have to admit it - I found myself kind of puzzled.

Then yesterday I went out to breakfast with my buddy, and the whole situation snapped into focus. Scanning the menu, I happened to notice the section that said, "Senior Specials – 55 and Over." And it dawned on me that I qualify.

That's it then. I'm a "Senior." Not only do I get to spend the next couple of weeks popping Motrin and hobbling around like Igor in some "B" horror movie, I can now order a breakfast that comes with just one strip of bacon. I can get a discount at theaters. I can have a bus boy help with my tray during the Early Bird Special at the

Old Country buffet. All I have to do in return is wear a hat whenever I'm driving the car, and leave the turn signal on.

What does it all mean? Well for one thing, I'm beginning to suspect that my sore back has less to do with that piece of paper and more to do with the cumulative effect of a whole lot of "No Guts, No Glory" decisions I made over the years. Mickey Mantle, the great baseball player, once said, "If I'd known I was going to live this long I would have taken better care of myself."

The Mick was one of my earliest heroes (I even insisted on being called "Mickey" when I was a kid, until a cute little black-haired girl in my third grade class told me that she thought "Michael" was the most beautiful name she ever heard, signaling the first time in my life that I gave a crap what cute little black-haired girls might be thinking). But I never took the slugger's words of warning seriously.

Instead, I have spent my entire life launching into each new scheme with the words, "Hey, what's the worst that could happen?" After that it was just a matter of being patient while whatever got sprained, strained, broken, cut, torn, abraded, contused or dislocated healed up. In fact on the plus side, all the time I spent convalescing gave me plenty of opportunity to cook up the next scheme.

But now that I'm officially able to order from the menu where everything comes with a side of prune juice, it seems like just thinking about doing a sliding dock start on a pair of pizza boxes makes my knees hurt. Maybe it's time for me to come up with a new life plan. Maybe it's not too late to start taking care of myself, to start being a mature, sensible adult. Maybe I should approach each day with caution, fully aware of all the potential risks. Maybe I should start planning right now for a rewarding and uneventful old age.

Hmm, I'll bet I really could do a sliding dock start on pizza boxes...

This Just In - Humans Are Only 95% Chimpanzee!

I just finished reading about a study that concluded that humans and chimps have less in common genetically than anyone had previously thought. It seems that a biologist named Roy Britten at the California Institute of Technology has used his computer and whole bunches of numbers to demonstrate that the genes of humans, once believed to be about 98.5% identical to those of chimps, are in fact only about 95% the same.

What a relief!

Here we sit at the top of the food chain, feeling like we have a pretty good handle on where we fit in the world (top of the food chain…), and along come a bunch of latter-day Charles Darwins trying to use their precious 98.5% figure to prove that we really are descended from apes, just because chimpanzees have more genetic material in common with the human species than your brother-in-law. These evolutionist swine were always happy to throw the statistics in our faces. "98.5%," they would giggle, "Have a banana, Monkey Boy!"

They were always using their "science" to argue against the obvious fact that mankind was created in one afternoon from a handful of mud, a couple of twigs and some duct tape.

Ok, I know what a lot of you are thinking, that Jennifer Lopez is really pretty good-looking, even though her image is sleazy and her music is completely derivative. But those of you who are still paying attention to this column are thinking that the difference between 95% and 98.5% isn't all that big of a deal. How wrong you are.

It's 3.5%!

3.5% is enough to account for opposing thumbs, which virtually define human endeavor. Without opposing thumbs, chimps can't hold a cell phone, build civilizations, unfasten a bra strap with one hand, hitchhike, juggle three running chain saws, or properly grip a handgun.

3.5% was enough to give Michel Lotito of Grenoble, France the imagination to go boldly beyond the chimp's mundane diet of leaves, vegetables and the occasional cockroach. He chose instead to eat (this is true) bicycles, supermarket carts, TV sets, chandeliers, a coffin, and a Cessna aircraft. Being French, Lotito probably ate all this stuff slathered with béarnaise sauce, but still…

3.5% was enough to let mankind move out of the primitive forests and circuses where chimps live, and move to subdivisions where we are free to mow the grass and throw potlucks without having to pick the lice out of our neighbors' hair.

3.5% is enough to let us stop hanging out in trees, foolishly foraging for food and swatting flies. Instead we can build cities and factories to produce miracles of technology like deodorant, SUVs, cheap firearms, bra straps that can be unfastened by anybody with an opposing thumb, global warming, leaching landfills, nuclear waste, and acid rain.

3.5% is enough to let us develop spoken language so we can recite poetry, sing songs and shout obscenities at right fielders. It's also enough to let us develop rap music, so millionaires in baggy pants can shout obscenities at teenagers.

3.5% is enough for us to maintain a detailed record of human history. Unlike chimps, who are not even aware that they keep making the same mistakes their ancestors made, we humans have the ability to recognize and write down our mistakes each and every time we repeat them.

3.5% was enough for ancient men to grow beyond hitting each other over the head with sticks like chimps sometimes do. We've spent the past 25 million years technologically evolving so that we could develop really good weapons to inflict peace on our fellow man. I think we can all agree that there's hardly anybody more peaceful than somebody who's been blown to bits.

So I say thanks, Roy Britten, for letting us know that we're an additional 3.5% better than those pathetic chimpanzees.

Or at least 3.5% *different.*

Snow Day

As some of you know, I have a pretty cool day job at a small library. One of the best things about this job is that when the local schools shut down for bad weather, the library shuts down too.

I get Snow Days!

This means that any time there's a chance of snow on a "school night," I instantly become eight years old. I monitor every available weather forecast. I scan the western skies. I subscribe to a 24-hour online school closing advisory service. And then, of course, I do my "Snow Dance."

For those of you who live in Southern California, on Mars, or anywhere else Snow Days never happen, the Snow Dance is a highly personal ritual that can take many forms. My own version of the Snow Dance is performed as follows:

1. Put your pajamas on inside-out and backward.

2. Tape a nickel to a west-facing window, with Thomas Jefferson looking out (watching for the storm). There are those who believe that the nickel must be from the 1960s or earlier, because of the relative purity of the metal. This is silly superstitious nonsense – any nickel taped to the window will make it snow.

3. Tear up some notebook paper into small "snowflakes." Mead 3-hole punched with light blue medium-width lines works the best.

4. Hop around on your left foot, through every room in the house, throwing your paper snowflakes in the air and singing "Snow come and shut down all the schools" to the tune of the Beatles' "Why Don't We Do It In The Road."

5. Explain all this to your wife. A consultation with an attorney, a mental health professional, or both may be necessary at this point.

And when you finally get your snow day, here's how it goes:

6:45 AM – the guy on the radio reads off the list of school closings, and hallelujah - you're on the list! You roll over and go back to sleep.

10:45 AM – you wake up with a start , thinking that you're late for work. Then you relax as you remember that you have a whole day to accomplish all the personal things you're usually way too busy to get around to.

11:45 AM – you wake up with a start...

12:00 Noon – you go downstairs, have a bowl of cereal and a cup of coffee. Then you sit back with a notebook and a pen to plan your day around all the personal things you're usually way too busy to get around to. You flip the television on, just to check out the news and the weather update.

1:30 PM – you decide to get going on that list of personal things you're usually way too busy to get around to, right after you watch the last episode in the "Flipper" marathon on the Family Channel.

3:15 PM – you wake up with a start...

3:28 PM – you make your mind up to dive right into that list of personal things you're usually way too busy to get around to, right after maybe ten or fifteen minutes of Guitar Hero, since you never seem to get a chance to crank the old PS2 up any more, and besides, you saw an article somewhere that said that video games can help build hand-eye coordination, and it seems like some of that would come in pretty handy...

6:45 PM – your wife comes home from work and declines your invitation to a Guitar Hero

Death Match before you shut down the old PS2 and start planning dinner.

Ok, that's pretty much it; I should wrap this up and go now. A 1948 nickel just turned up in my pocket change, and I have to go dig up a roll of tape.

Just the Two of Us

My wife and I met on a blind date 34 years ago. We had lunch. We strolled around Ann Arbor, swapping biographical semi-facts and philosophical insights. I played my guitar and sang John Denver songs to her, while she convincingly pretended to enjoy them.

By the end of that date we were spouting love sonnets and declaring our mutual devotion to the heavens. We were Romeo and Juliet, only without all the poisoning and stabbing.

Our second date just happened to be on Valentine's day.

Just a little over six months after we met, we got married. We were terrific newlyweds. We didn't have much money, but we discovered that you could still have quite a bit of fun if you stuck to the cheap draft beer and the house wine.

I worked on polishing up those John Denver songs and learned some Paul Simon. She managed to remain fairly cheerful through it all, and took up macramé. Then along came Eric Clapton's "Wonderful Tonight," and nine months later our son was born.

The whole romance thing changes quite a bit once you have a child. Those nights we used to spend listening to some local band screaming out its interpretation of "Sweet Home Chicago," gazing at each other over glasses of cheap draft beer and house wine, turned into afternoons spent gazing at the kid over plastic cups of diet coke and enduring the sound of the five thousand or so video games in the Chuck E. Cheese, as they waged a kind of ear-shattering sonic warfare with a Muzak version of "Shake My Sillies Out."

We spent the next eighteen years working our way pretty much full-time through a parade of diapers, sippie cups, chicken pox, swimming lessons, bicycles, hockey tournaments, little league, viola lessons, braces, girl friends, strange haircuts, guitar lessons, snowboards, jet skis, driving lessons, cars and, ultimately, colleges.

And now he's moved away and it's just the two of us again. These days, what we really enjoy doing on long winter evenings involves sitting in our comfy chairs side-by-side in the living room and watching Family Guy reruns. Whoever manages to stay awake until 11 PM when the Daily Show comes on gets to pick out what flavor of juice we buy, the next time we go to Costco.

Romeo and Juliet have become Uncle Henry and Auntie Em.

Not only have we gotten all grainy and sepia-toned, we have become totally predictable. Each of us almost always knows what the other is going to say next. Luckily, we both also know that finishing the other person's sentence would be grounds for divorce. After more than thirty years she knows enough not to talk to me in the morning until I start to whistle, and I know that I'd better darned well do some whistling in the morning if I'm going to get any breakfast.

To a young person, full of passion and hormones, this may seem like a fate worse than losing cell service, but it's really not so bad. There is an indescribably warm and wonderful comfort in our relationship. She knows that she will always have me to explain (again) how to operate the DVD player, and I will always have someone who will put up with being called "Toots."

So this Valentine's Day my wife and I will probably do something romantic, like getting the vacuum cleaner repaired. We'll also try to get some other stuff done that we've been meaning to get around to, and we'll feel pretty good about it. Then maybe we'll go out and split an order of Shanghai Noodles.

But at some point we'll also line up some cheap draft beer and house wine, and we'll take the time to do a little bit of gazing - just for old times' sake.

An Homage to Snow Shovels

I love my snow shovel.

Ok, I'll admit that doesn't exactly rank up there with Tristan and Isolde (look it up) or Rachel and Ross (see "Tristan and Isolde" or "Monica and Chandler"). But some of us are just prone to simple passions. And here in Michigan, from about the third week of December through the third week of March, a snow shovel is a guy's best friend, the infantryman's rifle, Zorro's sword, Linus' blanket.

Every Midwestern man knows that his snow shovel is his winter lifeline. Without it, he could get completely snowed-in, trapped, and unable to provide his family with any of the basic necessities of winter survival, like Doritos and beer.

Now I'm not talking about "snow blowers," those gas-driven marvels that take the snow in my neighbor's driveway and hurl it majestically into mine. We winter purists look at snow blowers with a certain amount of scorn, as in "Where the heck do you suppose he got the money to buy that terrific snow blower?"

Over the years I've had many snow shovels. Some were flashy, with sexy names like Slush-Buster 3000, or Slop Chopper, while others were quiet, unassuming, even mousey. They had identities too, but I admit that I was often so coldly uncaring that even as I think back on the tender times we shared, their names escape me.

For those of you who have spent your entire lives in the tropics, trapped in the unending monotony of what we Northerners disdain with cries of "Oh yeah, well those jerks down there have to put up with hurricanes – occasionally," a basic snow shovel is nothing more than a good-sized rectangular tin plate, slightly bent then bolted to a stick. The idea is that snow is relatively light, so you want a large surface area to pick up a lot of the stuff with each scoop.

The obvious theoretical shortfall here is that whole "snow is relatively light" thing. There are about three days in every winter when the combination of temperature, humidity, dew point, barometric pressure, wind chill, UV index and terror alert level are perfectly aligned, and on those days the snow is as light as... well, as the purest driven snow.

On every other day of the winter, the snow is only light relative to a shovel full of bowling balls.

Nevertheless, we gamely attack all sorts of snow with our slightly bent rectangular tin plates bolted to sticks. We scrape, grunt, chisel and chop, building satisfyingly huge mountains of snow on each side of the driveway.

Sadly, a snow shovel never really seems to last very long. In fact, with the slightest scrape across bare pavement the front edge tends to peel back and mushroom, since the tin blade is just slightly softer than cream cheese. And once the front edge is really beginning to show the ravages of age, a guy just has to move on to a newer, younger, firmer model.

In the past few years the market has been flooded with "ergonomic" shovels, featuring handles that are bent to look just like the ones I've run over with the Dodge. This is to reduce back strain and to save wear-and-tear on tires.

With the bent handle you can push the shovel along like a little plow. It actually only moves one shovel-full at a time and pushes the rest off to the side, which basically accomplishes nothing. But it looks really cool.

So in the end we are true Northern men, wielding our snow shovels like swords of truth and justice, cutting a righteous swath of mostly-clear asphalt through the ravages of winter, so that we can go forth to provide our families with life-sustaining Doritos and beer. As we gaze down our cleared driveways between the hard-won mounds of piled snow, we swell with pride at our hard-working pioneer spirit.

That, or we're just too stupid to move South.

Here She Comes!

The current Miss Illinois, Katie Lorenz, just happens to be the daughter of a couple who are among my closest friends. This is pretty amazing to me - I've known this kid since the key to her ultimate happiness involved nothing more than clean diapers and a Blues Clues sippy cup.

Now, in less than two weeks, she will take the stage in Las Vegas with 51 other drop-dead beautiful young women and compete for the title of "Miss America."

Yikes! Think about it - out of 6,538,961 women who live in Illinois, Katie is the one chosen to represent the Land of Blagojevich in this year's Pageant of Pageants. And the thing is, she is absolutely the best choice they could have made.

Katie has made me completely update my ideas about the whole pageant thing. She is an incredibly warm, intelligent, talented, poised and articulate young woman. She is even totally unpretentious; when she's hanging out around the house, the only hint that she is not just another "girl next door" is the sash and jeweled crown.

I think a lot of peoples' opinions of the pageant world have been pretty heavily – and unfairly - biased by a few beauty queens who were maybe not the brightest lights in the parking lot; the stunningly homophobic Anita Bryant springs to mind.

Of course we also, too, spent the 2008 presidential campaign, there, with Sarah Palin, who was once "Miss Wasilla," there, don't cha' know. Governor Palin kept us entertained with her skill at what has been characterized as "Pageant Speak" - any time she didn't know the answer to a question, she would blather in circles around unrelated rehearsed talking points until she ran out of time. Or breath.

I'm not sure that the current "Reality Show" trend is helping the image much either. Earlier this year Katie and the other Miss America contenders spent several weeks together taping a show called "Miss America – Countdown To The Crown." It airs at 10:00 PM on TLC on the four Friday nights leading up to the Miss America Pageant. We have already seen the first two episodes.

The girls lived aboard the Queen Mary, where they ran a gauntlet of Reality Show Challenges - like a Jeweled Crown scavenger hunt, or an inflatable obstacle course with a giant Slip 'N Slide. Girls in bikinis, lots of water and soap bubbles - do you suppose a guy might have designed that one?

But they also got coaching from experts in various aspects of the pageant biz, then participated in mini-contests to test those newly enhanced pageant-biz skills. What I had never considered was how difficult all those pageant skills could be. I guess I just assumed that the whole deal would be as simple as tossing on the old swim trunks, then wandering out on the stage and letting the crowd and the judges have a good look-see. The only tough part would come later, playing the saxophone while tap dancing in a Wonder Woman costume.

It turns out that there is actually a very specific set of sophisticated techniques for doing things like strutting the runway in stiletto heels while looking graceful, holding all your major body parts somewhere near where people expect to find them, and praying that a strap doesn't break.

Not to mention the mental toughness it must take to keep that Miss America Smile lit up through trick questions, setbacks, sore feet, no sleep, cramps, and wishing that you could just go out and wolf down a whole cheesecake.

So I will be watching the Miss America program this year with a much greater appreciation for the whole pageant world than I have ever had before. I hope you will too.

Oh yeah - and don't forget to root for Katie; she'll be the pretty one.

The Real American Pastime

All right everybody, it's time to toss Sis, Mom, Granny, Cousin Elmer, Emmy-Sue and the young-uns into the old Ford pickup, grab a couple of cases of Budweiser, scream "Yeeeeeee-Hah!" and head on down in the general direction of Talladega…

NASCAR's back!

Last weekend, the Daytona 500 marked the beginning of a new season of watching Tony Stewart put Kurt Bush into the wall in turn four - or vice versa - and I could not be happier.

The National Association for Stock Car Auto Racing is an undeniably American sports institution. It was born in 1948 on the sand at Daytona Beach, Florida, when a bunch of mostly-retired moonshine runners decided to go out and swap paint on their post-war Buick, Cadillac,

Chrysler, Ford, Hudson, Kaiser, Lincoln, Mercury and Oldsmobile street cars.

For years NASCAR drivers would grab cars right out of the showroom, tweak the engines and tires a little, then hit the track. In fact, some of them would rent cars for the weekend - presumably remembering to scribble their initials in the little blank on the rental form to buy the optional collision insurance.

In those days you could go out to the track and see Junior Johnson or Fireball Roberts banging around in almost exactly the same car you might take into town on Saturday to go banging around in the IGA parking lot. I guess it was supposed to make you feel better about driving a car with a steering wheel the size and weight of a hula hoop.

These days, things have changed a bit. The cars you see every weekend running on the super speedways resemble your family ride about as much as an F-18 resembles a parakeet.

Every single part of a modern NASCAR race car is carefully engineered for racing, with the perfect balance of weight and strength. This is so the cars can turn lap speeds around 200 miles per hour, then crush like Coors Light cans and fly into a million festive pieces when they hit a wall.

Of course, there are other forms of auto racing. For example, the Indy-style open-wheel cars compete mostly on the same high-speed banked oval tracks as NASCAR, only they travel a bit faster and fly apart into more and smaller pieces.

And then, pretty much at the opposite end of the motor sports spectrum, you'll find Formula One. In Formula One the most advanced open-wheeled cars in the world run on intricate road courses, while NASCAR races mostly involve mashing down the accelerator and turning left.

Formula One drivers are relentlessly international, dapper little guys, with names like Jean-Jacques or Nigel, who speak at least eight languages fluently. Most NASCAR drivers are as American as a six-pack, with names like Kyle or Darryl, and some of them just barely speak English.

Now, I will admit that I am a huge fan of Formula One racing. But I have to say that if you have as much as a drop of American blood in your veins, you can not help loving NASCAR – especially those drivers. These are guys who will put their lives on the line and compete for millions of dollars, then hang out in the infield and eat corn dogs with their wife and kids. They will walk away from a major engine meltdown and wreck, then grin and tell the television interviewer, "Yep, she blew up real good."

Bear in mind that while modern NASCAR drivers might say "y'all" now and then and prefer a pitcher of whatever happens to be on draft over a magnum of Dom Perignon, in order to be competitive in their sport they are probably as well-educated in their own way as any mechanical engineer on the planet.

You know, I really could go on and on about NASCAR and my heroes, but I won't. You see, the Auto Club 500 is fixin' to start any minute now...

All's Well That Ends Well

I've enjoyed the privileges of being a city boy for most of my life. This means that I have developed lungs that will filter more than two million toxic substances out of the air (these toxins apparently wind up in my liver, where they can be flushed out with periodic substantial doses of alcohol).

It also means that I have had access to "city water."

Ok, I'll admit that this may not seem like a big plus when you sometimes have to push aside chunks of "city water" to get to the part you drink, or when you hear from the mayor that, "On the up side, no known bacteria could possibly survive in all that chemical pollution."

But at least you know that when you turn the tap, something resembling water is going to come out. And on the very rare occasions when it doesn't, you just have to wait a while until some guys in yellow-and-orange-striped vests come around and fix it. So you can imagine how disorienting it was when we moved into a house where we get our water from our own well.

I got a little nervous when, before we even moved in, they had to "test the well." You see, over a lifetime of ingesting countless meals in diners with names like "Scabby Joe's," I have developed a philosophy that when it comes to washing down a mouthful of mystery meat, you're better off just to shut your eyes and drink whatever the stuff is in the semi-opaque water glass with the antique lipstick marks. Reading any sort of pathology report on it would just lead to negative thoughts.

You can imagine how relieved I was when the news came back that our well was "certified." The only specific thing I can remember about the report was that there were "acceptable levels of arsenic" - always a plus.

And then I forgot all about the whole issue until the first time our power went off.

Let's put this in perspective. It's not all that hard to stumble around the house for a few days with candles or a flashlight, and most of us can live that long without television. But a well plus no power equals no water.

Now, you can always buy bottled drinking water. What's more, our old friend "beer" contains quite a bit of water to go along with its wonderful toxin-flushing qualities (see paragraph one above). The trouble comes when all that beer has finished its job, and the word "flush" takes on a very different, much more functional meaning.

And then there was the first time the well itself broke. No matter how patiently I waited, nobody showed up wearing an orange-and-yellow striped vest. Eventually I had to get in the phone book and find a well-fixer guy.

After the well-fixer guy came, my first problem popped up when he asked "Where's your well?" after which we spent the next half hour crawling around and searching in the bushes. Of course, I was really just keeping him company, since I had absolutely no idea what a well might look like – unless it had a bucket on a rope, along with a sign inviting us to toss in a coin and make a wish.

After we found the well, getting it fixed was fairly straightforward. All it took was a wheelbarrow full of money and a willingness to have an enormous truck parked in my front yard for a couple of days.

And now, years later, I'm an old hand at this whole business. I'm on a first-name basis with two generations of well-fixer guys, plus I know how to say some cool things like "holding tank" and "pressure gauge." I don't actually know what they mean, but I can say them. And that's a start.

There's Something About Spring

Ok, the ice is gone from the lake. The mounds of grimy black snow that have been stacked on either side of the driveway since December have melted away. Crocuses and tulips are poking their heads out of the dirt and sniffing around. We've harvested and processed this year's crop of slush nuggets.

For those of you who may have missed my ruminations on slush nuggets in years gone by, these are those little treasures, ranging from hub caps to panty hose, that accumulate under the snow all winter. They emerge as the snow melts, along with those crocuses and tulips, to provide us with a sure sign of spring -plus a fascinating study in social anthropology. You can just picture the saga of tender unrequited love and betrayal told by the discarded bar coaster containing the message, scribbled on the back in lipstick, "Jane Doe – 1-800-GET-BENT."

But what I really wanted to talk about is another, more insidious thing that comes out in the spring – skin.

It is my theory that people just naturally want to be naked. After all, we are born that way. In fact, from a certain point of view (specifically, the point of view of the average hormone-laden thirteen-year-old boy), everybody is naked all the time - just mostly, it's under our clothes. And we are all naked when we indulge in the most pleasurable experience possible for human beings - I refer, of course, to taking a shower.

So it's just natural that after spending several long months swathed in layers of thermal long johns and big wooly socks we all feel a need to unwrap ourselves a bit and air out some of that repressed skin.

This unveiling takes place in stages, since some people seem to experience more intense skin repression anxiety than others. On the first sunny day in March, you'll spot a teenage boy looking all bored and tropical in baggy shorts and a t-shirt, chatting with a couple of teenage girls in tiny skirts and tank tops. These early enthusiasts have apparently overlooked the fact that the actual temperature is 39 degrees, although their first clue would be that they can't hear each other talk for the chattering of teeth.

Given another month and thirty degrees, a lot more of us will start uncovering. For some of us – those of us who did not get to spend half of the winter in the Caribbean – this is often not a pretty sight. Those arms and legs that have been hidden from the sun since Thanksgiving radiate with a sort of fish belly pallor that can actually damage unprotected eyes.

But spring is short, and we'll soon have our wardrobes back in summer form. Before long we'll be treated to the sight of a hefty mom wearing a string bikini top and short-shorts, strutting through the parking lot while her teenage daughter hangs back in the car, desperately searching under the seats for something she can use as a disguise.

Maybe there are a few good things about winter after all.

Tax Time for the Fiscally Challenged

It's April. Tax time. May heaven help us all.

Ok, I realize that not everyone is as freaked out about taxes as I am. In fact some people appear to actually enjoy this annual rite of calculating the government's cut of your worldly possessions – specifically, this would be Certified Public Accountants, IRS employees, and Lunatics.

But a lot of people who are not direct beneficiaries of America's annual Fleecing of the Proletariat nevertheless seem to deal with tax time fairly well. They simply gather their courage, a sharp pencil and an envelope full of receipts, assemble the appropriate tax forms, and plow in. A few hours later they emerge, a bit gray and shaken perhaps, but grimly cheerful. They lick the envelope, throw on some stamps, and rejoin human society to wait for their refunds.

These are the same people who can recite for you, off the top of their heads, their house payment, their property taxes, and their cell phone number. In other words, people who are a lot more organized – or at least a lot more aware of their surroundings - than I am.

All of this goes beyond my just being bad with money, a trait for which I am legendary. I've been known to get out of a taxi and give my last ten dollars to a panhandler before I pay the cab fare. When I hire contractors I always get three bids, then I hire the guy with the highest bid and the coolest truck. I often leave a fourteen-dollar tip on a six-dollar lunch tab.

Paid, of course, from the envelope of lunch money that my wife pins to my shirt every morning before I go off to work.

I think my problem is that whenever concepts like "cash flow," "finance," or "budget" enter my consciousness, I go into a sort of seizure. My mind goes blank, and if there is any money in my wallet I give it to anyone who happens to be nearby, in exchange for investment advice or candy bars.

Luckily, my wife seems to be immune to my fiscal confusion. Every time I panic over how we could possibly keep our tax receipts and statements organized, she calmly puts a shoe box on the table and says, "Just throw any tax-related stuff in there." I never do it, but just knowing that the shoe box is there is reassuring.

So how does a fiscally-challenged person like me deal with my disability? Well, as I'm sure you've already figured out, I married a woman who has the patience and endurance to take care of me - one who knows how to count change, calculate fifteen-percent tips, and put lunch money in envelopes.

Long before I met my wife, I briefly dated a woman who was an accountant, but it didn't work out. After our first April together, she joined some sort of religious cult and was last seen with her head shaved, dressed in a bed sheet, and playing a tambourine in Central Park. A mutual friend, a psychologist, said she was suffering from PTSD – Post Tax-cripple Stress Disorder. I feel that, somehow, I may have been partially responsible.

Go figure.

Here We Are –
The Pilgrims' Pride

The car pulls into Great Aunt Ellen's driveway at exactly five minutes after eleven on a fine Thanksgiving morning. Since the moment the family left the house, an hour before dawn this morning, Todd Junior and Little Suzie have been passing the hours playing festive travel games, alternating between the traditional "Let's Make Little Suzie Cry!" and the ever popular "Mom, Todd's Making Me Cry!"

Before the car has quite rolled to a stop, Mom, Todd Junior and Little Suzie are out and sprinting for the bathroom. Dad, who apparently has a much larger bladder, joins Great Uncle Charlie and Uncle Fred in the garage where they are squatting on the floor and studying the directions for a brand-new turkey fryer.

Great Aunt Ellen has arranged fifteen fire extinguishers at strategic points around the garage. Now she's standing behind the men, explaining how a story she saw on the six o'clock news proved that frying a turkey in the garage is twice as dangerous as tossing a burning road flare into a bathtub full of napalm.

Grandpa is sitting in a recliner in the living room watching the Macy's Thanksgiving Day Parade on TV. Grandpa is wearing a flannel shirt, wool pants, two pairs of socks, insulated work boots, and long johns. Grandpa has adjusted the thermostat so that the air in the living room is hot enough to curl the wallpaper.

Grandma, Mom, Aunt Karen and Aunt Meg are in the kitchen making things like pumpkin pies and mashed potatoes. Aunt Meg had wanted to make a mincemeat pie, but Grandma reminded her that Uncle Stan is bringing his new girlfriend, and she's some kind of a vegetarian, and insisted that they stick with pumpkin.

Before long Todd Junior has drafted Karen's boy Sheldon and Aunt Meg's twins into a rousing game of "Let's Catch Little Suzie And Tickle Her 'Till She Pees!" In her seven years on Earth as Todd Junior's little sister, Little Suzie has developed the survival skills of a ninja, so she locks all four boys in the basement and settles down to play Barbies with her cousins Brittany and Pammie.

The men carefully lower the turkey into the hot oil as Great Aunt Ellen falls to her knees and pleads for salvation. Aunt Meg tries without success to convince Grandma that mincemeat is not really meat, and besides they're having turkey, which is really meat, so she doesn't see the problem. Aunt Karen becomes a little hysterical when she realizes that you don't get gravy when you deep-fry the turkey, but Mom and Aunt Meg calm her down by opening another bottle of White Zinfandel.

Carl the Dog, lying on the floor next to Grandpa's chair, suffers a heat stroke.

And then, at last, the feast is ready. Uncle Stan and his girlfriend Stacey show up just as Great Uncle Charlie brushes the last of the white fire extinguisher stuff off the turkey and fires up the electric carving knife. After a fairly intensive cross-examination by Aunt Meg, it turns out that Stacey's a veterinarian, not a vegetarian, and mincemeat pie would have been just fine with her – maybe even her absolute favorite.

As soon as Thanksgiving Dinner is over, Uncle Stan and Stacey excuse themselves to go celebrate Thanksgiving with Stacey's relatives. Grandma won't let them go to their second turkey dinner of the afternoon without sending along a huge ziploc bag full of leftovers.

The women all hug and kiss Stacey goodbye, then they go to the kitchen to clean up the dishes and discuss what a selfish skank Stacey is to drag Stan away from his family on Thanksgiving.

The men join Grandpa in the living room, where the paint on the ceiling is beginning to blister, and sprawl about in nests of couch pillows and perspiration to snore through a couple of football games.

Little Suzie traps Todd Junior and the other boys in an upstairs linen closet, then joins the girls to resume the Barbies marathon.

And all is right with the world.

Innovation for a Bold New World

Not too long ago I saw a television commercial for what has to be one of the most important industrial breakthroughs in human history. Even though major advances of this sort are not really the focus of my column, this is a development so revolutionary that I felt it was my duty to share it with you here, on the off chance some of my readers may have missed the press briefing.

I am talking, of course, about Tater Mitts.

Like the Segue scooter and Ron Popeil's Pocket Fisherman, Tater Mitts just might change forever the way we view the world around us. Tater Mitts employ an ingenious blend of state-of-the-art rubber dishwashing glove technology with some sort of coarse abrasive, to let the average person peel a boiled potato in less than eight seconds.

This stands in stark contrast to the twenty-five or thirty seconds it takes to peel a potato with archaic "knife" technology. To put this into some perspective, if you peel an average of just six boiled potatoes per day, Tater Mitts could save you nearly fourteen hours every year. That's enough to watch the entire first season of Buffy The Vampire Slayer, with time left over to change the line on your Pocket Fisherman!

And then there is the safety issue. As the Tater Mitts commercial dramatically points out, peeling potatoes with that old-fashioned "knife" is just plain dangerous. While a Google search failed to turn up any statistics on potato-related injuries for recent years in the United States, I think the Tater Mitts spokesman's one-word dissertation - "Ouch!" – really says it all.

All this got me thinking about the perceived state of technological innovation in America. For example, some people think that our auto industry is doing poorly because we Americans have lost our innovative edge. To those people, I say, "Pah! Just look at Tater Mitts!"

Of course if you want to talk directly about innovation in the auto industry, just look at the Hummer. Ok, I'll admit that a Hummer is about as well-suited to most civilian uses as a rocket launcher, burns fuel like an oil well fire, and looks a little bit like a dumpster with mag wheels. But a mother of two driving a Hummer can easily transport the kids plus enough groceries and ammunition for about nine years in the survival shelter. Think of the savings!

And don't think for one minute that American innovators have been resting on their laurels. Just look at the new, smaller and more efficient Hummer, the H3, which is designed to contribute more than 11.4 tons of greenhouse gasses to the atmosphere every year, bringing us just that much closer to our goal of enjoying our winters sunbathing in a beachside tiki bar at the North Pole.

So, any time that we as Americans are tempted to feel technologically inferior when we see a Hyundai self-destructing on the side of the road or a Japanese dancing robot, we need to stop and remind ourselves that we are the people of the Veg-O-Matic (which both slices and dices!), the Salad Blaster (highly compressed salad dressing at its finest), Ginsu knives that can saw tin cans in half (who could imagine that an Asian-sounding name could apply to something so all-American), Hummers, Tahoes, Expeditions, Durangos, Escalades... and Tater Mitts.

Our Voices Were Raised Again

What's it gonna take?
How many lives?
How many voices left unheard?
How many years?
How many tears,
Until the ones in power hear the word. *

Last weekend I had the privilege of standing on stage at the 2008 Concert for Lost Voices with some of the finest folk and blues musicians in the world - Josh White, Jr., Kitty Donohoe, Peter "Madcat" Ruth, the Unity of Ann Arbor Women's Ensemble, Guys With Guitars, and Cliff Gracey - making music for hundreds of people in my back yard and on boats across the lake.

And now here I am a week later. The chairs are gone, the sound equipment has been packed off to another gig, and the Scottie's Potties have been hauled away. As the lingering aromas of patchouli and Zingerman's beef brisket dissipate into the air over the lake, I am still staggering around the yard, cleaning the last few empty Dasani bottles and dazed ex-hippies out from behind the hot tub.

At last I have a few moments to stop and reflect on what happened here.

For one thing, this year we welcomed Madcat to our Lost Voices family. If you don't happen to be familiar with his name, he is acknowledged as one of the best harmonica players in the world. I can almost guarantee that you have heard his incredible work in recordings ranging from New Heavenly Blue in the 1960s (Nan and I have their album in vinyl), to several Dave Brubeck jazz records, to Ford commercials.

The experience of making music with a flat-out genius like Madcat is kind of hard to describe. He is so responsive to everything that is going on that even as you play the first note of some sort of improvisational idea, it seems like Madcat is on it and bringing it back to you, but with your thought completed and infinitely improved. He came on stage early in the Concert with my band, Guys With Guitars, and let me bill him in the program as Willy Wheezewell.

By the way, don't anybody tell Madcat that I called him a "genius." He hates it when I talk like that.

We also unofficially added Luna to the entertainment lineup. For those of you who have had the opportunity to attend just about any outdoor musical event around the Ann Arbor area during the past forty years or so, you have probably seen Luna. She is something of a local icon, tirelessly performing her own very unique dance interpretations in that strangely open space that always seems to exist between crowds and performance stages. Luna performs dressed head to ankle-length skirt in tie-dye, and Madcat, who was wearing a Luna-created tie-dye shirt, introduced her to the crowd as "my personal tie-diatrist."

Luna favored the audience and every one of the performers with her leaps and twirls for more than four hours. I'm not sure how she had the stamina – I could probably keep that up for about ten minutes before you would need to get me an oxygen mask.

My friend Cliff Gracey, who has technically assisted us with our music workshops since the very first one at the WJ Maxey Boys Training School, got on stage for his first appearance at the Concert and performed a fantastic set. Cliff is a fine guitarist and has a great voice - which made a nice contrast to mine when the two of us did James Taylor's "Steam Roller Blues."

The Unity of Ann Arbor Women's Ensemble expanded on their a cappella triumph from last year with a wonderful performance, even stoically overcoming the jolt of my joining them to sing "Down In The River To Pray."

Of course, Kitty and Josh, my sister and brother since the beginning of this whole adventure, were their magnificent selves. Kitty introduced cuts from her new CD, Northern Border, and shared the news that her award-winning song, "There Are No Words," has been chosen to be featured in a documentary about the 9/11 attack on the Pentagon. Coordinated with the release of the film, Kitty will perform "There Are No Words" at the televised dedication of a new Pentagon memorial on September 11 of this year.

Josh used a large portion of his set to lend his voice to the music written by the boys in our most recent music workshop at Maxey. This had particular impact on the Maxey boys who had come to work in the setup crew and who were watching the concert from one of the pontoon boats.

There were a thousand other wonderful moments in the Concert. Each one amplified the outpouring of generosity and concern from all the performers, from our sponsors – The Braille

Project, Westwind Communications, Zingerman's, National City, People's Express, Herb David Guitar Studio and Seek Within – from all the volunteers who gave so freely of their time and energy, and from audience and individual donors whose generosity will allow us to continue our work.

Thank you all.

In this column I have often talked about the details of our work with incarcerated and at-risk kids, and you can pretty much count on me doing it again in the future. If you want to find out more about Lost Voices, just check out www. lostvoices.org.

Chorus from "How Many Years," music by Mike Ball and Josh White, Jr., lyrics by the Maxey Boys – Copyright © 2006.

Dock Tales - Once Again Into the Briny Deep

Springtime around here involves a number of rituals. There is the *Baring Of Pasty White Skin* I documented a while back. There is the *Chipping Of Horrible Stuff From The Barbecue.* There is the *First Harley Past The Bedroom Window At 3:00 AM.* And there is the always exciting recitation of *Where Do You Suppose I Left The %$#@ Lawn Mower,* a favorite in our family for generations.

But by far the most harrowing rite we perform each year, an event we schedule as soon as we spot the first exposed belly button in the IGA parking lot, is the sacred Putting The Dock In The Lake.

Now for some people who put docks in lakes, this process is relatively straightforward - they go get the dock from where they put it last fall, and then they put it in the lake.

Can you imagine?

These people have docks that were designed and built by engineers – people who have some idea how docks should be built. All the parts match and they fit together as the designers intended, yielding years of easy installation and dock-walking comfort.

For me, the process is a little more complicated. In the first place, about half of my dock came with my house when I bought it. It was at least twenty-five years old, and had apparently been built and maintained by a troll.

The dock, not the house. The house was built by drunks.

After a year or two, my friend Tom, my son and I got the hang of tossing that baby out in the lake. (Again, the dock, not the house. Or, for that matter, the baby. What's wrong with you?) We knew what piece went where. We knew which poles had the bolts corroded into little lumps of slag, so that the only way to adjust the height was to prop beer cans under the feet. We knew which sections were perfectly good if you just walked on them very, very gently.

Life was simpler then.

Unfortunately, that original dock did not get us far enough out into the lake, so we spent the next twelve years scavenging from friends who were buying those nice new docks. They were happy to have us come over and haul away all the parts of their old dock that were too crappy to burn.

So now the dock goes far enough out into the lake to suit us, but it looks like it was assembled by a committee of trolls. Drunk ones.

We have at least four different widths of dock with four different styles of supports, and none of these components even remotely work together. This means that every thirty feet or so we've had to design a "transition," a connection between otherwise incompatible sections, carefully engineered by whacking on various parts with a hammer until they sort of fit together.

This process is very time consuming. It requires a lot of standing around in waders and staring at piles of stuff we vaguely recall from last year when we dragged the whole mess out of the lake, gesturing with beer cans that are on their way to becoming height-adjusters. This is followed by a great deal of whacking with hammers.

This year my neighbor, no longer able to participate in the annual dock gala, sat in his picture window and watched our most recent effort. In fact, I think he may have popped some corn and had a few friends over.

As we were finishing up and toasting our collective genius at the end of two days of work, my neighbor joined us, wiping good-natured tears of laughter from his eyes.

"You know," he said, "a couple of years ago you wrote in your column that you were going to label all your dock parts and take pictures of how they went together. Why don't you do that? It sure would save you a lot of time next year."

Now you would think we would follow his sage advice, wouldn't you? You would be wrong.

A Day at Club Mallard

Most of you know that we live on the shores of Whitmore Lake, Michigan – "Where the women are strong, the men are good looking, and the children spend every winter asking why the hell we still live in Michigan."

What you may not be aware of is that every Spring we also provide the headquarters for a sort of singles club. For ducks.

We call it Club Mallard. Sure, we also get a fair number of geese, and the occasional swan, but our clientele is mostly ducks. They come in about this time each year, hoping to find that "perfect someone" to spend... well, at least the next couple of weeks with.

Please don't bother writing me with comments like, "I assume that you are referring to the common Anas platyrhynchos, possibly the most recognized species of duck in North America," then going on to tell me all about migration patterns and mating habits. I don't know anything about that stuff, and I don't particularly care to.

What I do know is that regular old ducks, the kind where the guys have green heads, show up at my place in the middle of April, then hang out for the rest of the summer, trying to pick up chicks.

Ok, since "chicks" also refers to very young birds, male or female, I'll admit that "trying to pick up chicks" might not really be the best choice of words here. We're talking about ducks, not Cardinals.

Anyway, I'm not entirely sure why the birds always choose my place. We do have a bird feeder in the yard, which seems to be the duck version of a bowl of mixed nuts and a jar of hard boiled eggs on the bar. And we have a good supply of the essential elements of duck ambiance – water and other ducks.

So every afternoon the ducks arrive, usually in same-sex pairs. The females swim around discretely, nibbling on passing minnows and probably chatting about what brand of bill-gloss is more waterproof.

Things begin to get lively when a couple of males splash down, wearing too much cologne and hopeful expressions. After swimming a lap or two and scoping the situation, they get into a wing-flapping fight over who was the first to call "dibs" on the one with the long brown feathers.

While the females try to act oblivious to this roughhousing, if you pay close attention you'll see that their tails begin to gyrate whenever one of the males is looking. Ornithologists call this early mating display by the females "Shaking That Old Money Maker."

Before long, the fights subside and the ducks pair off. This is followed by a languid interlude in which the new couples swim around in gentle, almost romantic arcs. The females keep Shaking Those Old Money Makers, while the males quack nonstop about their exploits on the high school swim team and try to keep their eyes fixed on the females above the neck.

As more males arrive, they all attempt to get hooked up with the female with the long brown feathers, so more noisy disputes start up. At this point, while the two males are fighting, the female sometimes takes off with some other guy who apparently managed to convince her that his Escort is just a loaner from the Porsche dealership.

There are generally quite a few more male ducks than females hanging around, so there is always the potential for a bit of turmoil and turnover. Luckily, some of those extra males seem to be either a little bit limp-winged or just plain practical-minded - if you get my drift.

The action in Club Mallard really gets hopping late at night. I think they actually bring in a band on weekends, because we keep hearing the song, "Waaaaak Waaaaak Waaaaak Waaaaak Waaaaak," along with the classic, "Waaaaak Waaaaak."

For the last week or so I've been thinking of cashing in on Club Mallard by creating an online version. I think I'll call it "Hatch.com."

A Few Thoughts About
Father's Day

Father's Day is coming up. It is one of my favorite holidays, mostly because "dad" is by far the coolest job I've ever had. It is also a little bit sad for me, because my own dad died when I was a sophomore in college.

My dad was ancient. After all, he had patches of gray hair at his temples, and he was not even remotely able to understand the things that were really important in my world. He was a big, strong, clever, funny guy, and I really admired him. But in my eyes he was also pretty much over-the-hill.

He was forty-six years old, exactly ten years younger than I am right now.

I think about this quite a bit, and I have to admit that it confuses me. Am I really a whole decade more over-the-hill than my dad was? There are days when I really think so, especially when I accidentally catch a good look at myself in a full-length mirror.

It's a lot more likely, though, that what we're really talking about is the view through the eyes of a twenty-year-old who knew everything there was to know, and who fully intended to live and stay young forever.

But I think that in some ways my dad really was a lot older at forty-six than I was. When I was in elementary school, I was clothes-pinning baseball cards in the spokes of my new bicycle and envying my friend who had a newer one. When he was in elementary school, he was busy surviving the Great Depression.

When I was seventeen, I was howling and playing my guitar in a rock band - and fighting with my dad over the length of my hair. When he was seventeen, he was riding in the nose of a B-17 and looking through a bomb sight.

When I was forty-six, my partner and I qualified to make the first of five trips as adagio doubles competitors to the Water Ski National Championships. When he was forty-six, the cigarettes and alcohol he'd been using pretty hard for twenty years, probably trying to take the edge off of some of his memories, or to dull the pain of some of his disappointments, took his life.

I guess I learned quite a few lessons from my dad. I quit smoking when my son was born, hoping to see him graduate from college (I made it!) and even see his wedding day (not quite yet...). I also decided long ago that rather than using alcohol to medicate my disappointments, I would do what I could to either change or accept them.

Now I don't want to make it seem that my dad only showed me things that I should avoid. Among many other lessons, he taught me that I could wield language and humor as a powerful sword, that no matter now nasty or angry someone is, he can't hit you – at least not very hard – if he's laughing.

He taught me that a great big, tough old WWII veteran and ex-football player could really love a scrawny little kid.

So when Father's Day comes around, I try not to waste time feeling bad that I don't have anyone for whom I can buy a clever Hallmark card and a cordless drill. As sad as it is that my dad never got to meet his daughters-in-law or snuggle his grandchildren, he came out ahead of a lot of the other young men who served in the war, who never made it home to snuggle their own children.

Instead I just remind myself that for all my mistakes, I always tried to be the best dad that I knew how to be. And I take a few minutes to try to remember what it was like to have that gentle giant lift me up onto his shoulders, or the way he laughed at the first joke that I ever put down on paper, or even the way he always smelled like Camels and Aqua Velva.

And how lucky I am to have those memories.

Yet Another Foray Into the Jungle of Tele-technology

I need your advice.

Last week I got an email from my cell phone company, telling me that it was time to get myself a new phone. They seem really eager to send one along, absolutely free, if I will just agree to send them back a large check every month for the next two years.

How could anyone pass up a deal like that?

I probably should mention that the phone I have now is working just fine. And I'm still discovering things it can do - like download stock quotes in real time, or fly a fully-loaded Boeing 747.

Maybe I'm such a sucker for new technology because I've been around so long. You see, I can remember when I was a kid and my family got our first television set, one of the first in the neighborhood. It featured a microscopic grainy black and white picture screen mounted in a cabinet that was made by taking the wheels off of a box car and adding some mahogany veneer.

On a good evening you could get three channels, although sometimes the only thing to watch was a "test pattern." This consisted of a very technical-looking series of circles and numbers inexplicably surrounding the portrait, in profile, of a Native American wearing a feather headdress.

Back in those days, a telephone was a big black lump of bakelite with a thirteen-pound handset and a finger-busting rotary dial. We paid something like ten dollars a month to rent our telephone, since you were not allowed to own one.

I can still remember the stir of excitement in our house when the Phone Company (there was only one) announced the availability of new phones in "Designer Colors" – diarrhea green or cat-puke gold. My mom, hoping to match the shag carpet in the living room, opted for the cat-puke gold.

I marveled through the years at the never-ending parade of telecommunication miracles; extra-long cords that could reach into the next room for "the ultimate in phoning freedom," dials built right into the handset, and touch-tone phones. Later, in the 1980s, I had one of those early automobile-installed cell phones, a miracle of space-age engineering that could often sustain bursts of conversation for more than fifteen consecutive seconds and crush the suspension on a 3,800 pound Cadillac.

So I am still amazed and delighted that we citizens of the twenty-first century can all carry sleek little fully functional telephones around in our pockets. At this point I'm even having a fair amount of trouble getting wrapped around the idea that a lot of the current cell phones can show movies and streaming television, on a crisp color screen that is just about the same size as the one in my family's old Philco.

And this dizzying barrage of features offered by the new phones is exactly why I need a little help from my readers. I need you to send me an email – address it to mike@ipathetic.com - and tell me what you like about your particular cell phone.

You see, I'm thinking that maybe I should get a phone with a built-in QWERTY key pad, which is pretty much like the one you have on your regular computer. It's called that because QWERTY is the word you get when you fall asleep while you're writing your column and your forehead lands on the keyboard.

Or possibly I should get one with a built-in two megapixel camera, assuming that I had any idea what a "megapixel" is. Or what I would do with two of them.

Or maybe I should just settle for a slight upgrade to the phone I have - maybe one that will show animated color graphs of the stock market swirling down the toilet while it actually lands that 747.

Everything I Know About Boats – Part I

Ever since my remote ancestor Oog Ball sat by the water in front of his cave and used his stone axe to hack a birch log into a 21-foot Mastercraft, my family has been involved with boats. Over many thousands of years the Balls have enjoyed a proud tradition at sea, from Titus "Blisterfingers" Ball, the famous galley slave, to "Bilgewater" Ball, who served as ballast with Admiral Nelson at the Battle of Trafalgar.

Of course, all of my ancestors who came to this country arrived by ship - although since they were Irish, they traveled 5th class, which is often playfully referred to by the other four classes as "freight."

Now it seems like all this nautical heritage should make me some sort of an expert on boats, so I've decided to write a comprehensive guide to watercraft. I happen to live a long way from any kind of "big" water, like an ocean or a Great Lake, but I am fortunate enough to live on a Pretty Good Lake, and I'm familiar with the boats on it. For this reason, and in honor of my distant ancestor's close relationship with Lord Nelson, I'm calling my guide:

Bilgewater Ball's Guide To Stuff You Might See Floating On A Pretty Good Lake

Ski Boat - A "Ski Boat" is one of the most common craft you will encounter on the modern Pretty Good Lake. There will usually be a person in a bathing suit clinging to the end of a rope and hurtling across the water behind the Ski Boat. These people are participating in the sport known as "Water Skiing."

The object of Water Skiing when you're towing a man is to hope he falls down so you can laugh at him. The object of Water Skiing when you're towing a woman is to hope she falls down and dislodges parts of her swim suit.

There is a variation of the sport of Water Skiing, called "Tubing," in which the participants, male or female, are dragged along behind the boat, clinging to some sort of floating device, while the boat driver performs the most violent and erratic maneuvers possible. This continues until all of the participants' swimsuits and/or limbs are dislodged.

Fishing Boat - Fishing is by nature a quiet, contemplative sport. The modern state-of-the-art "Fishing Boat" has a 300 HP outboard motor that will take these fiberglass torpedoes just past the speed of sound. The theory here is apparently that if you can't actually "Catch" the fish, you can "Stun" them with your "Sonic Boom."

There are many other kinds of boats that can be used for fishing, including the rare and exotic "Rowboat." This was powered by two wooden "Oars." Using a Rowboat provided what was once known as "Exercise." Plus, they were more polite - a fisherman in a Rowboat was able to sneak right up behind the fish and then quietly invite them over for dinner.

Canoe - A Canoe is a long, skinny boat with two pointy ends. This Native American craft is familiar to us all from the poem Hiawatha, by Henry Wadsworth Longfellow, which goes;

> *Forth upon the Gitche Gumee,*
> *On the shining Big-Sea-Water,*
> *Such long hair had Hiawatha*
> *Big Chief thought he had a Daughter.*

Or something like that.

Much like a Rowboat, the Canoe is propelled by a wooden "Paddle." It is fairly common on any busy Pretty Good Lake to see canoeists performing the festive "Waving Of The Paddle In The Air" ceremony as the wake from a passing Ski Boat flips them into the water.

Kayak - This is the Inuit version of a Canoe, also propelled by the Paddle. Usually made of the traditional "Red Plastic" so common in the Arctic, the Kayak wraps securely around the user's body. For this reason, when a Kayak is flipped over by a passing Ski Boat, the "Waving Of The Paddle In The Air" ceremony is generally followed by the ritual "Holding Of The Breath And Frantic Struggling In An Upside-Down Kayak."

Next week in Everything I Know About Boats, Part II, we'll discuss Party Barges, Sail Boats, Nautical Crotch Rockets, and other Boats That Go Way Too Fast.

Everything I Know
About Boats – Part II

Last week we began an excursion into the
wonderful world of watercraft, exploring my deep
knowledge of boats, boating, and the dislodging
of women's bathing suits. Here, as promised, is the
second installment of:

*Bilgewater Ball's Guide To Stuff You Might See
Floating On A Pretty Good Lake*

Sail Boat – There are a wide variety of
"Sail Boats" indigenous to Pretty Good Lakes.
Among the smallest of these is the Sunfish,
which is essentially a pointed plank with a "Sail,"
a "Rudder" and a "Running Board." The Sail
catches the wind and moves the boat, the Rudder
steers the boat, and the Running Board shoots
up and hits you in the stomach to let you know
you've reached shallow water.

One of the most popular types of Sail Boat is the "Hobie Cat." Equipped with large sails and rigged for relatively high speeds, the Hobie Cat consists of two sleek hulls with a "Trampoline" in the middle for the sailors. The hulls are spaced wide apart to make it really hard to tip the boat over.

The object of sailing a Hobie Cat is to tip it over hard enough to launch the sailors off the "Trampoline" and into "Orbit."

The largest Sail Boat you are likely to see on a Pretty Good Lake would be the "Sloop," named for the meaty thud you hear when the boom swings around and knocks you into the water.

Pontoon Boat – These specialized craft are possibly the most common craft seen on any Pretty Good Lake. They are sometimes called, in a masterpiece of redundancy, "Float Boats," or in a masterpiece of understatement, "Party Barges."

In their simplest form, they basically consist of plywood attached to a pair of aluminum pontoons, with a motor strapped on. Since Pontoon Boats are very often used in "Party Barge" mode, there is usually some sort of railing added around the outside of the plywood to keep the members of the Party from wandering off the Barge and into the Pretty Good Lake.

While most people would consider a Pontoon Boat to be perfectly equipped if it has a set of lawn chairs and a six pack, a lot of them come with sun shelter tops, plush couches, stereos, toilets, GPS navigation systems, depth finders, and other comforts. This is to justify charging $25,000 for plywood attached to a pair of aluminum pontoons.

There is a recent trend toward putting large motors on Pontoon Boats. This is so that modern Pontoon Boaters can enjoy the challenge of trying to control a craft that runs like a rocket sled and handles like a floating bulldozer.

Personal Water Craft – "Personal Water Craft," also known as "PWC" or "$*^@% Jetskis, " are very fast and very agile. They are also inexpensive and easily transported on a trailer, making them ideal boats for people whose knowledge of the open sea comes mainly from taking showers and watching Flipper reruns.

Nautical tradition dictates that all PWC must follow navigational patterns ranging from "Completely Arbitrary" to "Wildly Erratic." This has in turn spawned a nautical tradition among owners of larger boats to stop occasionally so that they can clean the PWC owners off their windshields.

So there you have it, a fairly comprehensive list of ...*Stuff You Might See Floating On A Pretty Good Lake*. Of course, there are any number of related objects you will occasionally find bobbing about, including oars, canoe paddles, water skis, water skiers, bits of PWC, bikini tops and unconscious sailors.

Happy boating!

Regarding Fireworks

As we all know, the Chinese invented gunpowder. Being deeply philosophical thinkers, it did not take them too long before they saw how useful the stuff could be for transforming entire enemy armies into big holes in the ground.

As a point of reference, this was at about the time in European history when chucking a spear at someone you didn't much care for was the pinnacle of modern military technology.

After a while the Chinese decided that, even if you didn't have any bad guys around that you wanted to blow into bad-guy hash, you should still be able to have fun with your gunpowder, so they invented fireworks.

The original cultural idea the Chinese had for fireworks was that they could be used to terrify evil spirits and cocker spaniels, and for this they apparently still work very well. You almost never hear of an all-out assault by fire demons on a suburban American town during the Fourth of July Weekend.

I love fireworks, but I'm also a little bit frightened of them. I probably owe some of my fear to Scamp, the dog I had when I was little. At the first festive explosion anywhere in the neighborhood, Scamp would retire to my mother's closet and ride out the crisis in a shelter she would prepare for herself out of shoes and shredded sundresses.

As for myself, a child of the 1950's thoroughly trained in the advanced federal "Duck and Cover" technique of survival against nuclear attack, I could see the obvious folly of that dog's simplistic approach. Anticipating by many years our current Department of Homeland Security's breakthrough "Duct Tape and Visqueen" method of safeguarding the American public, I would make myself an impenetrable fortress out of a bedspread and some folding chairs.

Then a few years later, when I was about seven, I saw my first public fireworks display - an exhibition put on by a teenager named "Toby."

Toby was tall and skinny, with an occasionally squeaky voice. He kept his hair slicked back with Brylcreem to showcase the acne on his forehead.

He wore tight blue jeans with the cuffs rolled up above his white socks, and a white t-shirt with a pack of Pall Malls rolled up in the sleeve.

In other words, Toby was a living god. He stood in the parking lot of the IGA, leaning rebelliously against the fender of his almost-new 1957 Chevy, with a cigarette dangling from his sneering lips and a mysterious brown paper bag on the hood of the car. He caught my eye, then reached into the bag and pulled out:

A Black Cat Firecracker!

I knew all about Black Cats. My neighbor Chris, who was going into the third grade, had told me about this guy his older sister knew whose cousin's friend blew all his fingers off with a Black Cat.

And here I was, standing not ten feet from one. Too paralyzed with fear to run or improvise any sort of bedspread fort, I watched as Toby coolly took the cigarette from his lips, flicked the ashes on the ground, then used it to light the fuse.

He held the sizzling Black Cat in his fingers for what seemed like an eternity, then casually flicked it toward an empty parking space.

The explosion was deafening. I jumped about three feet straight up in the air and landed in perfect sprinter's starting position, ready for a dash to safety. But Toby's voice stopped me in my tracks.

"Hey kid," he screeched, "if you thought that was cool, just watch this."

I stood, transfixed by the idea that a living god who owned a Chevy would speak to one such as me, and watched him fish six or seven more Black Cats out of the bag. He held them in a bundle, twisted the fuses together, then lit them with his cigarette. After another interminable wait he tossed them after the first one.

They separated and seemed to explode in the air, in a staccato rapid fire concussion that washed over me like a wave. I stood, gasping for breath, looking from the shards of smoking black paper on the pavement, to Toby's laughing face, then back again. And then I found myself applauding helplessly.

I don't know how long it lasted. Toby entertained me with every combination of exploding Black Cats he could think of, while I watched in slack-jawed awe. I would cheer and clap after each death-defying stunt, then watch in breathless anticipation while he prepared the next one. Finally he paused, hefted his brown bag to estimate how much ordinance he had left for his other entertainment obligations, then pretended to look at an imaginary wrist watch. "Well Kid, I gotta go now. See you around."

I was too overwhelmed to speak, even to say "thank you," so I simply gave him one more round of applause while he bowed, jumped into his Chevy, and laid a double patch of rubber down on the pavement as he peeled out of the parking lot and headed up the street toward Valhalla.

To this day, every time I see a fireworks display, I like to watch the staging barge. I feel like if I squint real hard, I can see the silhouette of a skinny guy with a Pall Mall dangling from his lips, walking from charge to charge to make sure that each one will be even more entertaining than the one before.

And I always clap.

This Land Is Our Land

There is something I get to do on the Fourth of July that is even more fun than all the Ballpark Franks that will be ritually sacrificed to charcoal flames in our nation's parks and beaches and backyards. More fun than the bottle rockets that will set fire to many of our nation's finest picnic table umbrellas and halter tops. Even more fun than all the beer that will anesthetize the sunburned bellies of our nation's countless middle-aged revelers.

For about an hour on the Fourth of July I get to "be" Woody Guthrie at our local library's "We The People" program. This is a celebration of some of the great patriots in American history, and of the words and ideas they used to change the world forever. I get to sit with the likes of Thomas Jefferson, George Washington and

Benjamin Franklin. I'll sing about riding my pony in the Oklahoma hills, and I'll sing about how this land was made for you and me.

I love it that Woody gets invited to this gathering, because when he was alive some of the people who were sitting at the top of this country's political heap were not all that fond of him.

You see, Woody Guthrie spent a big chunk of his life traveling around America during the Dust Bowl and the Great Depression, some of the hardest financial times Americans have ever endured. He sang to and about the millions of people who were struggling just to keep their families from starving to death while living in the richest nation on the planet. A lot of his songs talked about the greed and hypocrisy that made it possible for something like that to happen.

As you might imagine, this did not always sit well with everybody – especially the greedy hypocrites. They labeled him a traitor and anti-American. They threatened him. They harassed him. And when he went ahead and wrote songs about that, they blacklisted him.

One of Woody's best loved songs, and one that I'll be privileged to sing on the Fourth of July, is "This Land is Your Land." In case you were raised on one of the moons of Jupiter and are thus unfamiliar with this song, it glories in the majesty of America:

> *This land is your land, This land is my land*
> *From California to the New York island;*
> *From the red wood forest to the Gulf Stream waters*
> *This land was made for you and me.*

And it goes on that way with some of the most stirringly patriotic lyrics ever written. But most people are not so familiar with the last two verses Woody wrote for this song, because they rarely get played:

> *In the shadow of the steeple I saw my people,*
> *By the relief office I seen my people;*
> *As they stood there hungry, I stood there asking*
> *Is this land made for you and me?*
> *Nobody living can ever stop me,*
> *As I go walking that freedom highway;*
> *Nobody living can ever make me turn back*
> *This land was made for you and me.*

You see, some folks aren't comfortable with those verses, because they suggest that "this land" might in some way be less than perfect. It seems that these people define "patriotism" as obeying, without ever thinking or criticizing, the nation's rulers. In the 1960s they even coined and believed in the phrase, "My country, right or wrong."

Some of these people think a "rabble rouser" like Woody Guthrie doesn't really belong in a lineup of great American patriots.

But I say that's exactly where he belongs. If men like George Washington, Thomas Jefferson and Benjamin Franklin had subscribed to the "My country, right or wrong" idea, we would all still be eating fish and chips, calling our elevators "lifts," and have some clue as to what a "crumpet" is.

To me real patriots are people who see that something in the land they love is not right, and are willing to devote their lives to changing it. Maybe they do it by writing a Declaration of Independence and fighting a desperate revolutionary war against the most powerful empire on earth. Maybe they put on the uniform of our country's armed forces and lay down their lives to defend her.

And maybe they sing songs about freedom of speech, or human rights, or the need for unions to stand up for workers against the forces of greed and corruption - because this land really was made for you and me.

Ask Dr. Mike - Ten Ways to Dislodge Those Pesky In-Laws

It's been a while since Dr. Mike made an appearance on these pages. In fact, my newer readers are probably not even aware that I actually have a PhD, a Doctorate of Tequila Shots conferred by the prestigious University of Tim Online. This makes me at least as qualified to solve your most difficult and sensitive personal problems as, say, Dr. Laura.

Well I'm back, and I'm still poised to solve my readers' most difficult problems with all the professional skill and sensitivity you've come to expect from a guy who writes jokes for a living. Today's mail is a bit unique in that it actually came from a real, live reader and so possibly represents a real, live problem. Go figure.

Dear Dr. Funny Guy,

Why I ought to rip your arm off and beat you with the bloody stump.

My in-laws moved in with us a couple of months ago and they are starting to drive me crazy. They eat at regular times, go to bed early, and believe it or not, they expect my wife and me to help out with the cost of maintaining the house!

As luck would have it, they own the house, but damn it, we were here first. Now I have to put my pants on before I wander down to the kitchen.

What can I do?

Sincerely,

Hate Covering Up Those Fruit-Of-The-Looms

Well Looms, you might try saying, "Beetlejuice" three times. If this fails (and it will – didn't you see the movie?) you may have to resort to more drastic measures to get rid of your in-laws. Here are a few suggestions:

• Start a home business in the back yard; maybe a skunk ranch or a freelance sewage treatment plant.

• Whenever you're around your in-laws always wear hockey gear, speak with a Russian accent, and begin every sentence with, "Look, I mean…"

• Get up each morning at 3:00 AM and run through the house screaming, "They're after us!

The giant fudgesicles are going to kill us all!"

• Complain to your father-in-law that the Slave Trade just isn't what it used to be, and that you can't sell the kids for enough money to cover the shipping.

• Tell your mother-in-law that you think she's a "pretty classy dame" and that she's probably a lot better in the sack than everybody says.

• Buy a cat. Preferably a cougar or a mountain lion.

• Announce that you're going to pick up "a little something to protect the family," then come home with a box of hand grenades. Please note, if your in-laws are NRA members, don't bother with this one – they'll think it's a great idea.

• Join a pagan cult and invite the whole gang over to your house for coffee. Then sacrifice a goat in the living room.

• Join a heavy metal rock band and invite the whole gang over to your house to practice. Then sacrifice a goat in the living room.

• When you're roaming around the house, don't worry about covering up those Fruit-Of-The-Looms. In fact, don't even wear the Fruit-Of-The-Looms. Maybe you could substitute a little number fashioned from duct tape and a sandwich bag. Trust me, nobody wants to see that - or even think about it.

I can pretty much guarantee that if you try all of these suggestions you will wind up with either a house that is completely in-law-free, or a restraining order. And if you happen to also lose your wife somewhere around the cougar or the pagan cult, just tell yourself that you now have just that much more room to sacrifice goats.

Thanks for writing.

Well that's it for this column. Be sure to send all your important, life-changing questions to drmike@learnedsofar.com. I may use them in some future column, giving you the deep satisfaction of knowing that you may have helped screw up somebody else's life.

Purple Haze on the Water

Yesterday we were on a boat belonging to my new friend, Mike. It was one of those cool "wakeboard boats" with a big chrome tower on it - the latest in tow boat technology. This tower is designed to provide the perfect up-force on the tow rope, so that a wakeboard rider can more easily perform tricks like the "Dum Dum" – which, as we all know, is an inverted toeside front roll with a backside 360.

Ok, we should get a few things straight here. First off, I'm not sure that my friend even owns a wakeboard. But if he does, I'd bet a lot that he is way too smart to ever attempt a "Dum Dum." Or, for that matter, any other trick the description of which might include a word like "inverted."

Just a guess.

I think a more realistic purpose for the chrome tower on his boat may be that it holds a pair of the neatest loudspeakers I've ever seen. These are "torpedo" speakers, meaning that if you set the radio at about three-quarter volume, a guitar riff will sink a freighter.

When I discovered a Jimi Hendrix CD in my friend's on-board collection, I convinced him that a few cuts from Are You Experienced would be an interesting way to demonstrate these speakers to those of us who were relatively new to the concept of tower-mounted audio marine ordinance.

As the first strains of "Purple Haze" began to re-liquefy the Jell-O shots in the cooler, I noticed an interesting thing – while the women on board smiled bravely and nodded their heads to the rhythm of the initial blast wave, every one of the guys stood up, treated each other to brief demonstrations of air guitar, and then began to closely scan the lake to see who might be noticing our show.

And when the occupants of a pontoon boat anchored about a half mile away signaled their enjoyment with a festive shaking of fists, we all exchanged high fives and some more air guitar.

So the obvious question is, why do guys act like this? I would hazard a guess that we may be looking at the same dim backwater of male psychology that makes a young guy put an $8,500 sound system in a 1989 Ford Escort he bought for $350, then thump his way through the mall parking lot, shedding his rear-view mirrors and other semi-critical auto body parts as he goes.

It's hard to believe that it could be any sort of male drive to attract attention to ourselves. If we had that kind of compulsion, we men would probably dress a lot better than we do. At the very least there would be no such thing as aloha shirts, novelty neckties, or Speedos.

And I would also rule out the idea that this might be some sort of demonstration of power or virility. Yes, I realize that gorillas will pound their chests and make a lot of noise to scare away rivals, but would a gorilla be able to appreciate the musical nuance of a guy picking a guitar with his teeth, then slamming it into the speaker stack to create feedback?

No, I think the most likely explanation is that we guys just feel a deep philanthropic need to provide much-needed entertainment for all the other, less acoustically fortunate people around us. You see, guys understand that the highest essence of humanity is sharing.

That, and the joy of setting off car alarms with your subwoofer.

How to Talk to Chicks

This morning before breakfast my wife lobbed a verbal grenade into my coffee cup. She asked, "What do you think of my friend, Brunhilde?"

(Please note, my wife doesn't actually have a friend named "Brunhilde." This is a sophisticated literary device, known in the trade as "Making Stuff Up.")

Now to a newlywed or a male Cro-Magnon, this Brunhilde question may seem like a perfectly normal conversation starter. To a man who has been married for almost thirty-three years, however, the peril is clear; there is no possible answer you can give that can't explode on you.

Here's how it works:

If you say the obvious, something like, "I think Brunhilde is great," there is a pretty good chance that you'll spend the next thirty minutes of your life hearing all about how Brunhilde is a two-faced trollop who can't be trusted. Then you'll get another thirty minutes discovering that you never stand up for your wife, and that you probably should just go right on ahead and run off with Brunhilde.

If, on the other hand, you say, "I think she's a two-faced trollop," you are likely to learn that you never have put one iota of effort into really getting to know any of your wife's friends, and that you have no right to be critical of a caring, lovely, misunderstood person like Brunhilde.

So, for those newlyweds and male Cro-Magnons out there, here is a partial list of ways to navigate the conversational minefields you are sure to encounter with your wife.

Wife: "I think my hair looks horrible."

Husband: "Mmmmrowm."

Wife: "My brother / father / mother / sister is an idiot."

Husband: "Drowfl!"

Wife: "How do you think a rich girl like Paris Hilton gets all those men to buy jewelry and cars for her?"

Husband: "Nnnnngong."

I think you can easily see the pattern emerging here. In fact, the most successfully married guy I know has not said an intelligible word in his wife's presence since the early spring of 1966.

For those of you who feel some sick need to engage in or even initiate actual conversation with your wives, here are just a few things you probably should avoid saying:

"I think I really owe it to myself to have another couple of beers before Jack and I head out to the golf course."

"If you were just a little better organized, I'll bet you could get all that laundry done before you go to work."

"Geeze honey, you think maybe you should hit the old Stairmaster?"

"Hey, you know that girl I used to live with in college? Well, I ran into her yesterday, her divorce is final, and she's looking great!"

"How drunk do you suppose a guy would have to be before he could choke down a plate of this tuna casserole?"

Of course, a woman can get away with saying pretty much anything she wants to a man. Almost every married guy should be thoroughly accustomed to hearing things like:

"You aren't going to wear that shirt, are you?"

"Your brother / father / mother / sister is an idiot."

"Are you really going to eat another pork chop?" or the corollary, "Why don't you go buy some pants you can get that fat butt of yours into?"

"Have you been sleeping in a dumpster? Go do something with your hair."

"I'll bet Dave Barry's wife doesn't have to trip over six pairs of Dave's shoes in the living room..."

Ok, maybe that last one is just me.

Anniversary

My wife and I celebrated our wedding anniversary on Saturday. We've been married thirty-three years; that's twelve thousand and forty-five days. Actually, twelve thousand and fifty-three, if I've managed to calculate the leap years right.

This means that my wife has had to listen to me singing the first verse (the only part I know) of Bob Dylan's "Buckets of Rain" something like seventy-two thousand, three hundred and eighteen times, a feat of endurance that some experts feel ranks right up there with surviving the Spanish Inquisition or a Neil Diamond concert. Personally, I think I at least partially broke her spirit sometime in the mid-eighties.

From time to time in these pages I've shared some of the secrets of my marital success, most recently in a culturally sensitive column entitled, "How to Talk to Chicks." A couple of years ago I even documented my attempt to get my wife to sign a pre-nuptial agreement, thirty-one years after the fact, so I could protect the assets I brought into the marriage (a guitar and a 1968 VW micro bus). From time to time in the future, you can count on me to share additional deep insights.

But the real secret is very simple; marry your best friend.

Ok, don't bother writing to tell me something like, "But Mike, I'm a straight guy, and my best friend's name is Chuck." I'm not talking about the person you most enjoy hanging out with when you're drinking beer and pretending that there is even the slightest possibility that the hot young blonde in the string bikini might be even remotely interested in either one of you.

I'm talking about the person with whom you are willing to share everything, from all your cash, to a dessert at the Big Boy when you're just a little low on all that cash, to the only "spork" they threw in the bag with your bucket of chicken and mashed potatoes. The person who will gently nudge you awake just before you slide out of your chair and onto the floor at the oboe recital. The person with whom you actually enjoy going to oboe recitals.

We celebrated our thirty-third anniversary by buying some take-away sushi, a bottle of wine and a bouquet of flowers (because we all know how much I covet fresh flowers!), then enjoying a sushi and wine picnic in our living room while we watched the Detroit Tigers game on TV.

We were living large!

We could have spent a bunch of money on champagne and filet mignon in a romantic restaurant. Some day, if we ever happen to come by a bunch of money, we might just try that. But probably not, because take-away sushi, wine and the Detroit Tigers in our living room are among the things we like best.

Since the day we got married, me wearing an open-collared shirt and a sport coat and she wearing a flower-patterned peasant dress, my wife and I have pretty much marched to our own drummer. We have generally had things to talk about, and yet we have always been comfortable with the idea that sometimes one or the other of us just might not feel like talking.

It's not that our marriage lacks romance. It's just that our version of romance has never exactly been the kind of stuff that you would expect to see in a Fred Astaire and Ginger Rogers movie. We almost never spontaneously break into Gershwin songs and tap dancing routines.

No, the basis of our romance is that we both dearly love hard-checking forwards in Red Wings uniforms, and Ernie Harwell's voice describing a guy from St. Claire Shores catching a foul ball (we miss you, Ernie!), and going to the Ann Arbor Art Fair, and skipping the Ann Arbor Art Fair, and sitting on the boat and watching the sun go down, and raising emotionally-challenged cats, and grilling a package of whatever happens to be on sale at Polly's Market, and eating take-away sushi…

And each other.

Selling Crap

I've come to a decision - I'm going to sell all my crap.

This has not been an easy thing for me. All my life I have been a compulsive "crap saver," meaning that I'm the kind of guy who can't bear to throw away those little plastic hanger dealies that you get when you buy new socks, or the small Ziploc bags that the screws from the stereo cabinet came in, or really nice shoe boxes. So I have a really nice shoe box full of small Ziploc bags with some of those little sock hanger dealies in them.

I have years worth of empty pill bottles. I have slide rules from high school. I have at least three drawers full of "mystery keys." I even think I have a pair of two-tone purple patent leather and suede platform shoes that I've been saving since I got beat up and thrown out of a disco in 1975

- probably for wearing two-tone purple patent leather and suede platform shoes.

So this Purging of Possessions is really a pretty new thing for me. And what, you may ask, is behind my sudden anti-accumulationist reformation? I can give you the answer in a single word;

CraigsList.

Ok, back in the days before the WorldWideWeb made word spacing unfashionable, that would have been two words, but you get the idea. Craigslist is an online classified advertising Web site that posts more than thirty million new ads and receives more than nine billion page views every month.

Here's how it works: if you have some crap and a computer, you can take pictures of your crap and use your computer to upload them to Craigslist. Then anybody who wants to acquire some crap can look on Craigslist, find your crap, and buy it from you. And the best thing about it is, it's all free!

Craigslist has categories for pretty much any kind of crap you might want to buy or sell; furniture, musical instruments, motorcycles, jewelry... you can even use your computer to sell your computer on CraigsList, which is pretty cool when you think about it - kind of like running out of pork chops and eating your own leg.

Of course there is another incredibly popular internet buy/sell service, called eBay, where you post pictures of your crap and people all over the world bid on it in an exciting virtual auction. This is different from a live auction in that with eBay you wind up with a lot less shouting and a lot more Doritos crumbs in your keyboard.

Craigslist is more straightforward. Your ad just sort of sits there quietly waiting for someone to discover your crap, then send you an email to ask if you're willing to take 93% less than your asking price.

Since Craigslist basically operates locally, you end up having a good old-fashioned conversation with your potential buyer in which he tells you that he can't afford to pay what you were asking for your crap because he needs to hang onto enough cash to pay for his grandmother's surgery. You then explain that selling the crap for 93% less than your asking price will just not give you enough money to pay for that reconditioned crutch you've had your eye on.

Finally you come to a consensus. Money changes hands, the buyer goes away happy, and you look around for more crap to take pictures of.

That crutch isn't going to buy itself, you know.

The Dark Side of Craigslist

Last week I talked about selling all my crap on Craigslist . In the process of doing that I have discovered that not everyone on the World Wide Web is completely honest.

I know. It shocked me too.

Here's how it went. I listed a 12-string guitar on CraigsList, and along with other replies I got this:

"Hey, I just went through the ads you have on here on Craigslist and it's actually what i wanna buy, i will like to purchase these item from you, hope it's still available for sale... either way it goes, i am always online so you can email me back."

Ok, his word choice is a little bit unusual, and his shift key is apparently broken, but at least the tone is friendly. I assume that he could not spell the word "guitar" or copy it from the subject header, but I thought "these item" got the point across well enough. I sent a reply:

"Yes, the guitar is available. I'd be happy to let you have a look at it."

After a couple of days I got this:

"Thanks for the prompt response, i'll like to make an instant purchase right away, i will send a draft via my bank to cover the cost as am satisfied with the item. I will need the details of whom & where to mail the draft. It will be delivered by the United Parcel Service within 2 days. Please note 'ups' do not deliver to P.O. Box addresses. The require detail needed are : Name to be on check, Address to deliver the draft and your phone number should in case i might have someone call you on my behave because i am deaf. Kindly delete the posting as am totally committed to buying from you to save me cost, above all, you don't need bother about the shipping i will have my mover come for the pick up as soon as you have get the payment."

Ok, while it seems encouraging that he'll like to make a purchase not only "instant," but also "right away," I noticed a couple of curious issues here. For one thing, a cynical person would wonder why someone who might have someone call me "on his behave" because he is deaf would want a guitar.

Plus, while I am happy that he is totally committed to buying from me to save him cost, it seems like sending a bank draft by UPS is a fairly odd way to carry out what should be a fairly simple financial transaction. And even though a 12-string is large for a guitar, it probably would not require a "mover" to pick it up.

Finally, I'm not entirely sure how he would have come to be "satisfied with item," since we have never exchanged any information about it. In fact, the actual word "guitar" still seems to elude him.

So the question you have to ask is, what is going on here? After a little research I found out that this is a classic set up for a fairly common scheme in which a buyer, who for some reason can't deal with you in person, commits to buy something sight unseen at your full asking price.

After a few days a bank draft shows up written for several times the cost of whatever you're selling. The buyer asks you to refund the balance by wire transfer, usually letting you keep a little extra for your trouble.

The punch line comes a couple of weeks later when the bank informs you that the original bank draft is phony. Apparently certified and cashier's checks are among the easiest things to counterfeit these days, since the bank will accept them without question, then hold you responsible when they turn out to be worth just a little bit less than fiberglass toilet paper.

So here I sit, disillusioned that such dishonesty could dwell in my fellow CraigsListers. The one bright spot is the email I got yesterday. It seems that I have been chosen to help a widow in Nigeria get 14.5 million United States Dollars out of Africa, keeping ten percent, or 1.45 million United States Dollars as a commission.

Good thing – I haven't sold the guitar yet, and I could use a little extra cash.

Try Not to Step in the Metaphor Droppings

I recently swapped a trumpet that I haven't played in nearly forty years for a used guitar. This guitar is a sturdy, no-frills, great-sounding thumper that will be perfect for taking out on the boat or tossing in the luggage rack of an airplane. The brand, a respected Canadian make which will be familiar to most serious guitarists, is Seagull.

Ok, here's where it gets funny. Sort of. I absolutely *hate* seagulls.

I should point out that I was in college in 1970, and like every other philosophy-addled undergrad of the time, I read Richard Bach's Jonathan Livingston Seagull with slack-jawed fascination. I was so taken by the lone soaring bird as an allegory for life and aspiration that I had a seagull as part of the logo for my company for more than twenty-five years.

And then I moved to the lake, where I discovered why the very nicest thing lake dwellers ever call seagulls is "rats with wings."

It turns out that a single 14-ounce seagull can, in a single day, produce something like 43,560.17 square feet of seagull poo. It also turns out that each of these precious little feathered metaphors considers it a personal mission to spread their acre of excrement all over my stuff.

There is something chemically unique about seagull poo. When it's fresh, it sports a consistency and odor that could nauseate a maggot. It also contains a bonding agent stronger than the NRA's love of carnage, since you can't blast the stuff off a canopy with a power washer.

I have to admit that cleaning up after the gulls usually turns out to be a fairly interesting biology experiment. Since seagulls will eat pretty much anything (including Doritos, ice cream cones, stray jewelry, and smaller seagulls), they tend to leave behind a fascinating crapalistic record. The occasional wad of pooped-out bones from some unfortunate little seagull brother or sister stands as mute testimony to the struggle for survival between nature and our feathered feces-flingers.

I also have to admit that the things we come up with in our attempts to keep the seagulls away from our stuff have often been pretty entertaining. We've tried cutting pie tins into strips and hanging them about like some sort of demented tinsel. We've tried fiber optic geysers sprouting at intervals from canopies. We've tried brightly colored pinwheels.

My favorite is the Fake Owl, which actually does work - for about a week. The gulls are a good deal smarter than me on this one, because after two years I still find myself grabbing the binoculars and calling the neighbors to see the owl sitting on my hoist.

So by now I've pretty much given up on all of the passive poo-bird repulsion methods. These days, any time I look out and see the dock, boats and hoists covered with a layer or two of seagulls, I just grab two boards and run down the dock, screaming and clapping the boards together. This does make them take off, in a cloud of fowl-smelling feathers and digested Doritos. And they stay away, at least for a few minutes.

I think even rats with wings know enough to keep their distance from a crazy man.

Never Cared to Say Goodbye

As some of you know by now, there is a benefit concert coming up at our house on Labor Day. If you haven't heard about it, you can get all the details at www.lostvoices.org. To give you the short version, Josh White, Jr., Kitty Donohoe, Robert Jones and some other friends of mine are going to join me to make music to raise money for Lost Voices, a group that works with incarcerated kids. We'll use our deck as a stage and perform for a whole lot of people on the lawn and on boats.

I discovered that the one problem with having a party for, say, hundreds of people, is that my wife is not necessarily all that keen on the idea. I discovered this when she handed me my pillow and suggested that I sleep in the shed for the next few months. She apparently feels that the house should be tidied up a bit before all those people get here. I tried to calm her down by putting on my best Johnny Cash voice and saying, "What's the big deal, Baby. It's just a little old concert."

When I came to, I was sort of folded up on a pile of gas cans in the shed. And my wife had apparently changed her mind about letting me have the pillow.

It took some serious negotiation and personal groveling before we were able to reach a compromise. She finally agreed that we could have the event here, on the condition that I would spend every moment until the day of concert either working on some aspect of cleaning the house, or unconscious in the shed.

A couple of my friends, as soon as they heard about my situation, immediately offered to help me "muck out the place." A quick trip to the dictionary revealed what every horse owner already knows - that "mucking out" is the process of shoveling poo out of a stall. Now I am aware that over the years I have accumulated a pretty fair amount of poo here in my stall, so I decided to take them up on the offer.

It never occurred to me that my friends might take a sort of sadistic pleasure in the whole situation. They would hold up an item I haven't laid eyes on in years - like my favorite fishing rod with the tip broken off and the fish line caked with rust from what was left of my favorite reel – and coldly suggest tossing in the pile headed for the dumpster, never heeding my pleas of, "But they make kits so you can fix that kind of thing..."

And my wife has not been any more sympathetic. She likes to narrow her eyes and say things like, "So exactly when do you figure you're going to need this cracked goalie stick, considering that you've never played so much as one minute of goalie in your life?"

And so I've been watching helplessly as some of my favorite possessions – in a very real sense my prime poo – have gone into the garbage bags that would bear them out of my life. Last night I woke up in a cold sweat, dreaming about the discarded paper bag of leftover screws and washers I had been saving since the early eighties when I first assembled the late, great gas grill, Carl.

Sometimes you just have to grit your teeth, wipe away a tear, and let go.

Mindy

Cats are kind of strange.

I guess this will come as a surprise to absolutely nobody. For people who don't much care for cats, it probably goes a long way toward explaining why they... well, don't much care for cats. And for those of us who inexplicably do like the fuzzy little maniacs, I guess it is at least one of the reasons why we do.

It's been a while since I've talked about my cats here. We're down to two now, Libby, a.k.a. "The Phantom," and Mindy, a.k.a. "I'm Not Fat, I'm Just Fluffy." Aside from my wife and the vet, nobody living has actually seen Libby for a couple of years. I know she's real, though, on account of the steady conversion of money to cat food then to stinky litter, with an occasional vet bill thrown in.

Mindy is, unfortunately, a little under the weather. A while back she developed some sort of itch in her right eye, so she used her cute little kitty claws to shred that eye to kitty burger. The vet does not recommend de-clawing a cat as old as Mindy, so she did the next best thing. She put an "Elizabethan collar" on her.

Now, I've been around cats all my life, and like most cat lovers I've happily experimented with any number of ways I could use to piss them off. Up to this point, trying to give them a bath was the hands-down winner, followed closely by coaxing them lovingly into a pet-carrier – have you ever tried to stuff a cougar into a cigar box?

I'm here to tell you that this collar explores whole new levels of cat pissed-off-ness!

The Elizabethan collar is a flexible blue vinyl cone thingy that ties around the cat's neck and keeps her from getting her paws to her face. This serves to provide the cat with unimaginably increased incentive to get her paws to her face.

In the four days since we put the collar on Mindy, it really seems to be doing its job. We've been treated to ninety-five hours of hissing and baleful looks, along with methodically clawing the collar to shreds (I think she passed out from exhaustion for an hour or so yesterday).

And despite the fact that the little sweetheart has discovered the substitute therapeutic procedure of bashing her face repeatedly against a door frame, she just can't quite get her claws on that eye, and so it is starting to look a tad less kitty burger-ish.

I've tried to imagine how frustrating it would be to have something like that Elizabethan collar put on me, especially if I was not able to really comprehend the reason for it. I might wonder if I was being punished for something. Or I might feel as if the people I loved and depended on for everything in my life were simply trying to make me miserable. In either case, I think I might be pretty angry with those people.

Fortunately, Mindy does not seem to feel that way. She knows darned well that I am personally responsible for that collar being on her, and despite all the hissing and baleful looks she still crawls up on my lap for a little comfort.

I guess that's what real trust is all about. It seems like she has decided that as much as she hates that stupid collar, and as incomprehensible as the whole situation may be to her, I must have my reasons for putting it on her. And she won't waste one moment holding a grudge.

Maybe people should learn to be as strange as cats.

Sitting on a Stool at the Counterculture

My friend Mary recently showed me a photo she took on vacation. It's a close-up of a blue sign with white letters, painted on steel and a little rusty around the edges, nailed to the wooden siding of a cabin. The sign says, "Hippies Use Back Door – No Exceptions." There's also an arrow presumably pointing to where the Hippies might find the back door, letting us know that the sign means to provide navigational instructions rather than a lifestyle suggestion.

I'm not sure whether to be amused, insulted, or maybe just a little bit flattered. Having spent my teen years wandering through the 1960s, I'm not ashamed to admit that I was a hippy then, and that I am still an unreconstructed hippy at heart.

Of course, the same might be said for pretty much everyone my age who is not a Fox News personality or serving somewhere else in the Bush administration.

So how do we define a "hippy?" I think Timothy Leary said it best in his 1967 book The Politics of Ecstasy; "Hippy is an establishment label for a profound, invisible, underground, evolutionary process. For every visible hippy, barefoot, beflowered, beaded, there are a thousand invisible members of the turned-on underground. Persons whose lives are tuned in to their inner vision, who are dropping out of the TV comedy of American Life."

Of course, in the next chapter Dr. Leary reminisced about a three-way argument he once had with a bag of pretzels and a shovel, over whose turn it was to drive home.

For me and my friends, being a hippy was never really all that political. It was more about seeing how long you could grow your hair before the assistant principal nabbed you, gave you a dollar, and sent you across the street from the high school to the barber shop, "Bob's Buzz Cut Emporium."

That, and about girls who didn't wear bras.

Then of course there was The Band. I was a member of a five-piece garage (that's where we practiced) rock band that probably enjoyed more success than musical ability. Like every other band in the '60s, we worked hard to cultivate our wild, free, counterculture image.

Somewhere around the house, carefully hidden from my impressionable son (ok, he's 25 and probably not all that impressionable any more, but he could still be emotionally scarred), there is a photograph of The Band, taken for some sort of promotional thing. In this photograph we are posing on somebody's rooftop, the drummer hilariously using the brick chimney as his drum kit. We are all scowling at the camera in what is either brooding musical genius or the aftermath of a trip to White Castle.

And there, front and center, stands a pathologically scrawny me, wearing a headband, a tank top, and hip-hugger bell-bottom jeans with peace-sign patches on the knees and at least two feet of flare at the feet. My Fender guitar is slung low and covered with hand-painted peace signs and flowers. My hair is blonde, stringy, and approaching that universal happy hippy goal of shoulder-length - indicating that when the picture was taken it had been some time since one of those involuntary trips to Bob's.

Looking into the photograph at my whiskerless face, you can almost see the spirits of Jimi Hendrix, Janice Joplin and Jim Morrison surrounding me. You can almost hear them whispering in my ear that I should let my Freak Flag fly, that I should go out and stand up against The Man, that I should use my music to strike a lasting blow for Peace, Brotherhood, Love, and Freedom - just as long as I could save up enough energy to join the Revolution after studying for that Biology test coming up next Monday.

No wonder they wanted us to use the back door.

An October Afternoon
in Manhattan

Emerging from Penn Station with their wheeled luggage rattling along behind them, a balding and vaguely frightened-looking father speaks in excited German over his shoulder to his bewildered wife and their two young sons, who are in total sensory overload. His fanny pack is turned to the front to help him avoid becoming a victim of American crime, probably a helpful tip taken from the Reiseführer New York City paperback book sticking out of his back pocket.

She has long brown hair, and she is considerably less than five feet tall, even in her spiked high heel shoes. She is pretty in that cute-but-shy-girl-you-knew-in-high-school way, striding along with her eyes firmly aimed at the pavement. Her life strategy at the moment is to keep moving, and above all never make eye contact. She is not afraid, just smart. The portfolio under her left arm might contain her artwork, or her head shot, or her lunch.

He walks up 32nd Street directly in front of me, wearing a long gray cloth coat, faded blue jeans, new-looking work boots, and a black leather civil war cap. A reddish pony tail hangs down his back and a wispy red beard flares out on both sides. As he marches along, he carries on an animated conversation with an invisible friend.

Two middle-aged Hasidic men in their black wool suits, flat-brimmed black hats, and untamed beards stand at the stop light, waving their arms and shouting at each other in Yiddish. The tone of the conversation is not angry – just loud. One of them clutches a bright red Macy's bag. The other one holds up an index finger to call a temporary time out, then answers his iPhone.

They are the best dressed couple among the Water Taxi passengers, young and beautiful and tanned and black-haired, wearing lots of gold jewelry and cologne. He has the craggy good-looking face and amazing nose of a Native American. She speaks with a faint Spanish accent. They've brought along their very tiny baby daughter in a stroller for the one-hour tour up the East River, hoping to get a peek at the Statue of Liberty and the Staten Island Ferry.

They tell the Water Taxi Tour Guide, an animated young black man in Reeboks and a Yankees cap strutting around the front of the boat and rhyming his Water Taxi Tour Guide speech into his cordless microphone, that they are from New Mexico.

She is tall, at least a quarter Asian, and breathtaking. The tail of her green plaid flannel shirt sticks out beneath her tight waist-length black leather jacket, forming a kind of skirt over her black tights. Tooled brown cowboy boots and a blood red handbag complete a look that reflects either fashion genius or a broken mirror at home.

The two young men sitting at the tiny round table in the Starbucks window touch each other a little too often and a little too fondly for them to be just guys who like to watch the Giants games together. They are completely oblivious to the mocha-scented world around them, and it is oblivious to them.

She shuffles along, her ancient slippers like a pair of sky blue flocked ice breakers pushing aside the occasional cigarette butt or crumpled Lunch Buffet Special flier. Her moth-ravaged fake fur coat leaves only her bare pale-white ankles exposed. It is not all that cold, but she has a bright green wool scarf wrapped around her neck, trapping her carefully brushed gray hair. She stops at a card table by the curb where two young

Hispanic women are soliciting donations to feed the homeless, then drops a twenty dollar bill and a handful of pennies into their thick-glassed big green bottle.

This day like every day, the cosmos of Manhattan, tinged with the scents of street vendor kielbasa and bus fumes, touches and swirls past these people - and 7,999,983 others. It never pauses, and it never passes judgment.

Welcome to the real Real America.

The Gospel of Guy Food

Last weekend was my wife's birthday, so I wanted to surprise her and make dinner. I thought long and hard about it, and I prepared the perfect menu for the occasion:

- Steak
- Beer
- Cake

Then I had second thoughts. My wife is, after all, a nurse, and she is very much in tune with issues like nutrition and a balanced diet. I revised my menu to include all the essential food groups:

- Steak
- Beer
- Cake
- Hot Sauce

Not necessarily in that order. Oddly enough, when I served the meal, my wife did not seem entirely satisfied. For one thing, she doesn't like beer, and it didn't seem to make her feel better when I offered to help out and drink hers. But I knew it was more serious than that when she screwed her face up into that cute little "I can't believe I married this moron" look and said, "Where are the vegetables?"

"Aha," I said, holding the bottle of hot sauce triumphantly in the air. "Right here!"

"How do you figure?"

"Well, catsup is a vegetable, and this is kind of like catsup. Only hot."

"Since when is catsup a vegetable?"

"Since the Reagan administration."

Like Ronald Reagan's Secretary of Agriculture, I eventually lost that particular argument.

I really don't understand my wife's ideas about food. She bases her bizarre concepts of diet and nutrition on the advanced diet and nutrition courses she took in nursing school, along with a lot of subsequent reading and study.

I, on the other hand, have developed and refined my culinary knowledge through many years of practical hands-on experience, standing around the yard with a beer in one hand and a barbecue fork in the other. That, and watching beer commercials.

Picture in your mind a typical beer commercial featuring a bunch of young, good looking guys sitting around with a bunch of young, good looking women, enjoying a young, good looking campfire, drinking beer, and toasting their youth and good lookingness.

Now picture what they're eating. I'm thinking steaks, or ribs, or maybe some burgers and brats. It's a pretty safe bet that they are not letting the good times roll with little watercress sandwiches and puree of broccoli. I have developed a very simple set of eight cooking rules that I live by, and I offer it here as a nutritional model for men everywhere.

1. If it doesn't fall through the grill into the fire, and it's not zucchini, it's good. Just as long as it's not zucchini.

2. A leaf of lettuce and a slice of tomato on your hamburger counts as a salad. A slice of onion sort of counts.

3. "Hops" are little green leafy thingies. A lot of green leafy thingies are vegetables. They put hops in beer. Therefore, beer is a vegetable.

4. Potato chips are vegetables. Don't let anybody tell you any different. Add onion dip with chives, and you have a vegetable medley.

5. Never make a casserole. Ever. It's ok, maybe even mandatory, to eat the casseroles prepared by your wife, but initiating one without provocation could cost you your Guy License. This is because many casseroles include ingredients that could be grilled (see rule number 1 above). Chopping these up and baking them in a dish with mushroom soup is an abomination of nature.

6. When it comes to seasoning, if a little bit is good, a lot is better. If it makes you sweat and brings tears to your eyes, it's great.

7. There is no flavor problem that can not be resolved with Tabasco.

8. No zucchini.

Love is Not Hard to Find

She wore a baggy purple shirt over baggy purple sweat pants. Her hair was chopped short and her body was padded with a layer of soft flesh that bore tribute to the starchy diet of incarceration. She had her arms folded across her lap, her gaze fixed on the floor in front of her, and she was almost imperceptibly rocking to a rhythm that only she could hear.

She was maybe sixteen years old.

I can't use her real name here. Let's call her Krissy. I have no idea how she came to be locked up. It is not a question we ever ask. We can safely assume that at some point in her short life everything just spun out of control, to the point that it no longer worked for her to be out in the world.

Kitty Donohoe and I were at the Adrian Girls Training School in Adrian, Michigan conducting a Lost Voices roots music workshop with Krissy and eight other incarcerated teenage girls. The idea was to help them turn some of their personal poetry into folk and blues music, and to work together to write some music as a collaborative group.

Krissy's speech was slightly impaired. When we eventually got her to look up from the floor, she announced that she was "... not too good with words. Not like those smart girls. Not like those pretty girls." She was fairly certain that Kitty and I would never be interested in what she had to say, an assumption based on the fact that not many people in her life ever had been.

So we encouraged her, but we told her that she didn't have to do anything she didn't want to do. As time went on she contributed to the group song, "The ATS Blues." And she listened supportively to the work of the other girls.

One day when Kitty and I arrived at the workshop, just about every square inch of Krissy that wasn't covered by baggy purple shirt and sweat pants was covered with bright red scabs. She didn't mention it, so neither did we. After the session the Staff member from her cottage told us that over the previous weekend Krissy had rubbed most of her skin off on a piece of carpet.

A couple of weeks later Krissy was mostly healed up - at least visibly. She smiled at the floor as she handed me a creased piece of lined paper and said, "I wrote this poem." I stopped her before she could go on to say that it was probably not very good.

Here's Krissy's poem, after Kitty and I helped her tweak it so it would fit the music a little better:

Love Is Not Hard To Find
You can find it in the midnight sky
In the music of a baby's cry
Love is not hard to find
You can find it in a quiet place
In the beauty of a friendly face
Love is not hard to find
You can find it in the wildest storm
Or when you're sitting safe and warm
Love is not hard to find
You can find it in a tender song
Or when you know where you belong
Love is not hard to find
You can hear it on a city street
In winter cold or summer heat
Love is not hard to find
You can find it big, you can find it small
Find it anyplace at all
Love is not hard to find
Love is not hard to find.

We put Krissy's song to a sort of Calypso tempo with a bright melody to match. When she first heard her words carried on the wings of Kitty's incredible voice, she was amazed. When we told her we were going to use her song as the grand finale of the kids' performance at the end of the workshop, she was thrilled. And when she heard the ovation it earned she was overwhelmed.

But the very best moment was just after the show ended, when we were all standing around the stage basking in the afterglow. I caught the sound of a group of the other girls from the institution, who had come to watch, singing and clapping time as they filed out of the auditorium.

I looked at Krissy and said, "Hey. Hear that?" She tuned her ears to the sound of those other girls - those smart girls, those pretty girls. Then she turned back to me with a look that made everything I have ever done for Lost Voices worth it, ten times over, bathing me in the most beautiful smile I have ever seen.

Those girls were singing, "Love is not hard to find, Love is not hard to find, Love is not hard to fiiiinnnd!"

What Happened to Indiana Jones?

I am not really all that good at getting out to see movies in the theaters. It's not only that I don't like paying $15 for tickets and $11.50 for a bucket of popcorn saturated with bright yellow motor oil. I've just never been all that wild about the way my sneakers stick to the concrete floor under the seats.

So I just got around to renting the DVD and watching the latest Harrison Ford movie, Indiana Jones And Something Or Other About Some Kind Of Skull. Now I don't normally write movie reviews, but I feel that in this case I need to share my considered thoughts on this film, especially for the benefit of any of you who have not yet plopped down $3 to take it home and see it.

Don't do it! This movie stank up my house worse than a goldfish under the sofa cushion!

Just in case any of you didn't understand that delicate simile, I will explain; I did not care very much for the film.

From the opening scene with its obnoxiously computer-generated prairie dog, past Cate Blanchett sporting the worst Russian accent in show business history, through a jungle full of obnoxiously computer-generated monkeys, and right up to the Indiana Jones Hat Gag just before the closing credits, I sat and wondered if maybe Steven Spielberg and John Lucas shouldn't consider hanging it up and buying a fishing charter business in the Bahamas. Even the John Williams music, with that wonderful "Bam-pa-da-pa, bam-pa-da" Indiana Jones theme, couldn't save this thing.

And Harrison Ford couldn't save it.

I will admit that I have had a bit of a man-crush on Harrison Ford ever since he blazed like a comet across my television screen in his role as "Beach Patrol Cop" in that memorable 1968 episode of Mod Squad. Years later, when he sat at the controls of the starship Millennium Falcon wearing the same dopey look on his face that I get when I can't remember how to eject a CD from the car stereo and said, "I have a bad feeling about this, Chewie," I knew that we were in the presence of true motion picture greatness.

Harrison Ford was even fairly... well, Harrison Ford in this latest movie. Ok, his hair has quite a bit more gray in it, and his voice has gotten kind of Jim-Beam-with-beer-chasers gravelly, and it's apparently getting a lot harder to make the stunt men look like a guy who is 66 years old. But he still has the whip.

I'm not entirely sure why this movie was so bad. I loved the first three Indiana Jones movies unconditionally, despite lines like, "Listen. Since I've met you I've nearly been incinerated, drowned, shot at, and chopped into fish bait. We're caught in the middle of something sinister here..."

In fact, I can watch and enjoy some incredibly silly movies. I've seen *Young Frankenstein* so many times that I can recite most of the dialog:

Dr. Frankenstein: "Frau Blucher?"

Horses: "Whinny!"

And it was actually pretty nice to see Karen Allen back as Indy's love interest, reprising her Marion Ravenwood role from Raiders of the Lost Ark. I enjoyed a rare moment in motion picture history in which the leading lady does not look like the leading man's granddaughter's best friend.

The problem might be that Indy isn't truly

Indy any more. He used to be a middle-aged guy who could throw a punch like most middle aged guys secretly believe they could if they really had to. He sort of stumbled through his life without any sort of long-range plan - which is really not all that unusual I guess, except most of us hardly ever have to whip up a spur-of-the-moment escape from Nazi Germany in a Zeppelin.

But I think what we all liked best about Indy was that he was always curious (and courageous) enough to grit his teeth, push that nasty old mostly-rotted corpse out of the way, and stick his hand into the spider hole.

Now we have a character on a motorcycle, who turns out to be Indy's long-lost son and who barely adds up to a parody of *Rebel Without A Cause*, calling him "Gramps." The main theme of the new movie seems to be that Gramps can still throw that punch. Except it turns out that every time Gramps took one in the chops, you could almost see the Polident flying through the air. This time Indy just didn't work.

So when "Junior" (if you saw the flick, I'll bet that you didn't know, or care, that the kid's name was supposed to be Mutt Williams) went Tarzan-swinging through the jungle while giant ants ate a bunch of the bad guys, I found myself hoping he would fall and go the way of those bad guys, just so we could get it over with.

Oh well, I guess that's why they make air freshener. At least my sneakers didn't stick to the floor.

Japan - Part 1

As I'm writing this I'm sitting in a big aluminum tube 32,000 feet above the Bering Straits, hurtling through the air at more than 550 miles per hour. The person sitting in the economy class seat in front of me apparently suffers from some sort of affliction that makes him lunge violently backwards every few minutes, driving his headrest into my forehead, my tray table into my belt buckle, and my belt buckle into my spine.

The guy across the aisle from me has been sniffling and hocking up chunks of lung since we left Detroit. The woman next to him appears to be suffering from a touch of cholera. There is a rumor that bubonic plague is spreading through Business Class. I've been in this ballistic Petri dish for four hours, and I'll be in it for at least another nine.

And strangely enough, I'm up here on purpose - I'm on my way to Japan.

Whenever someone finds out you're going to Japan, they right away want you to bring them back something. Maybe a DVD player, or a Samurai sword. Or a Honda. One of my friends asked me to bring him a Geisha. In each case I had to explain to them that there was no way I could get any of that stuff in my carry-on. Well, maybe the Geisha.

Then, once we established the idea that I probably won't be cramming a duffle bag full of Japanese women into the overhead for the return trip, my friends would turn into Charlie Chan. "Ahhh, sooo," they would say, wittily squinting and bowing and making buck teeth, "You honolable numba one son!"

"Charlie Chan was Chinese," I explain. "At least he was supposed to be. I think the actor who played him was an Irish guy from Baltimore."

"Ahhhhhh sooooo, velly solly!"

Which brings up the issue of language. I don't know, but I'm pretty sure that bowing and squinting and substituting "l's" for "r's" will not quite make it in Japan when it comes to, say, ordering a hamburger or giving a deposition in front of a grand jury.

With this in mind, the first thing I did to prepare for the trip was to try to learn a little Japanese. I got a big, impressive set of CDs and books with a name on the cover something like Mastering Japanese in Ten Days or Less.

I learned quickly that this name was only accurate if, before buying the CDs and books, you did a little preparation – like being born to Japanese parents and raised in Japan. So, after a bit of shopping I found a language course book more my speed – Get Your Face Slapped in Sapporo – Japanese Phrases for Americans and Other Morons. From this book I learned that "Good Morning" is "Oh-Hieo-Goziamas," and "I'm Sorry" is "Gohm-Mehn-Nasai."

After that, my head exploded, so I decided to only speak to Japanese people from 6 AM until noon, and to be very sorry at all times.

The next challenge was packing for the trip. Like, how much stuff do you take along when you're going to spend eleven days in a place where you won't able to ask a store clerk how much a toothbrush costs?

Then there was the issue of money. Changing Dollars for Yen is pretty cool at first - for $100 you get ¥11,000! This is great until you discover that a cup of coffee in Japan costs about fifteen billion Yen, and that you need a Swiss bank account to afford a full dinner.

So here I sit, with my belt buckle imbedded in my pancreas, with more Yen than I can count in my pocket and God knows what stuffed into the suitcase that I checked in Detroit and is probably happily winging its way to Denmark.

Next week: how to eat a squid with chopsticks. And why anyone would want to.

Japan - Part 2

Ok, so here we are in Japan. We've come here to fly my friend Scott's balloon in the Saga International Hot Air Balloon Festival, an event designed to introduce top balloon teams from all over the world to the idea of eating raw squid.

It seems like everything you eat in Japan involves raw squid. If you buy a traditional Japanese meal, it includes at least one plate of it. If you order a steak, you get a side of it. I kind of expect my next cup of coffee to come with cream and two raw squid cubes.

I'm not really sure why these people eat so much raw squid. I think it may have something to do with an ancient Japanese philosophy that the key to a long, healthy life is eating stuff that the rest of the world would only use for bait.

There are two major kinds of Japanese raw food; sushi, which is strips of raw fish or meat wrapped up in or plopped on top of a chunk of rice; and sashimi, which is just strips of raw fish or meat. You dip your sushi or sashimi in a mixture of soy sauce and wasabi, which is a kind of green horseradish paste that is designed to blow the back of your head off. Then you pop the whole thing into your mouth and make "yummy" noises while the wasabi blows the back of your head off.

And as far as I can determine, there is nothing that the Japanese won't eat. Yesterday we went to a restaurant that specializes in unagi. Unagi means "eel."

This was a place where you could pay your respects to your soon-to-be lunch, still slithering around in a big tank with a lot of other eels. The lunch, not you. While we were there we enjoyed a special delicacy served between our eel salad and the eel entrée – fried eel bones. The trick to eating fried eel bones is to smile and crunch on them loudly while you try to forget that what you're eating is fried eel bones.

The Japanese people are a small race, and they are rarely overweight. This is because they don't overeat. And they don't overeat for two reasons: First, considering the kind of stuff they find on their plates, they don't really want to. Second, they use chop sticks.

You know, it seems like the people who invented the samurai sword and the Toyota might have also been able to come up with silverware.

The secret to eating with chopsticks is to hold your plate up close to your mouth and tap on it with your chopsticks while you lap the food up with your tongue. If you can establish a steady spray of rice and raw stuff hitting the walls, floor, and ceiling, you're on the right track.

While the Japanese do not eat a lot of food, they more than make up for this when it comes to consuming alcohol. They even have a special phrase to describe the Zen of drinking, pronounced "jyun kaitsyu," which basically means drinking yourself into a stumbling, slobbering stupor. You reach the perfect Zen state at the exact instant you pass out face down in your plate of fried eel bones.

It's time to go now. I have a plate of squid sashimi waiting for me and a fair amount of jyun kaitsyu I'd like to catch up on.

Next week – all these idiots are driving on the wrong side of the road!

Japan - Part 3

The first thing you notice when you hop into your rental car in Japan and try to drive it away is that the gas, brake and clutch pedals are missing, and you're sitting there trying to steer the glove compartment. And for some reason the front seat passenger gets a steering wheel.

I discovered that there were also pedals on the passenger side, and that all the Japanese people seemed to like sitting over there when they drive, so I figured, what the heck. When in Fukuoka...

The Japanese also seem to really enjoy driving on the wrong side of the road, like the British do. I think this might have something to do with the amount of tea both British and Japanese people drink – it's like all that caffeine makes them want to grind their teeth and make right turns into the left lane.

Driving in Japan presents a number of challenges beyond shifting gears with your left hand and remembering which lever is the turn signal and which one operates the windshield wipers (I never did quite master that). For one thing, the roads are all narrower than the mind of Pat Robertson, and they all allow two-way traffic. Add in pedestrians, bicycles, and the Japanese habit of building houses and rice paddies right up to the edge of the road, and you have a driving situation that makes bungee jumping seem relaxing.

Oddly enough, the Japanese do not seem to get particularly stressed by all of this. In fact, just to make things a little more interesting, most Japanese cars have little television sets mounted next to the steering wheel, angled so the driver can dodge around school kids, talk on the cell phone, and still catch the latest episode of Bowling for Sushi.

Just a side note here on Japanese television – they have some of the most creative ads I've ever seen. And even though they speak a language that seems to consist of beautiful but entirely random sounds, you can generally figure out exactly what they are selling.

My favorite was a pitch for some sort of cold medication, viewed as a gaggle of schoolgirls dove for the relative safety of a soybean field. In the commercial, a samurai master is explaining the value of concentration to his young pupil and holding up a bottle of the medicine. In the next scene, as the young warrior is engaging in a sword battle, he sneezes and loses both the battle and his head.

Talk about clearly establishing the need for the product!

The hardest part of driving in Japan comes from the fact that very few streets have names, and the ones that do are called something different every few blocks. Plus, nobody has a street address, which means that the normal state for most Japanese drivers is "rost."

We spent our first three days in Japan driving around hopelessly rost, a problem compounded by the fact that we couldn't read any of the signs. And whenever we encountered Japanese people who spoke enough English to help us, even they had a lot of trouble finding any place they had never actually been to before.

And so my greatest victory as a motorist in Japan was the first time I recognized a 7-Eleven (yes they have those in Japan) I had seen before, and was able to successfully navigate back to where we were staying. I pulled triumphantly into the driveway, only three and a half hours after leaving a restaurant five miles away, with my windshield wipers signaling my turn for all the world to see.

In my joy of accomplishment I shouted, "Banzai!" which I believe is Japanese for "Hey everybody, the Meathead finally made it home!"

Next week – we don't need no culture; we're from Detroit!

Japan - Part 4

I'm going to go way out on a limb here, and say that most Japanese people look a lot alike.

Now before you start sending me nasty emails explaining everything that is terrible about what I just said, please read on. Then go ahead and send me those nasty emails - I enjoy pretty much any attention I can get.

Anyway, the thing I found most striking during the time we spent in Japan was that we were visiting an island where virtually all of the inhabitants are members of a single race. We were in Saga, which is a moderate-sized city in a very rural area, a long way from the international influences of Tokyo. Saga is kind of like the Japanese version of Fort Wayne, Indiana; it will probably never be considered the cosmopolitan epicenter of the nation. Any nation.

But you would be hard-pressed to walk through any shopping center in Fort Wayne without seeing a mix of white, African-American, Hispanic, and Asian people, not to mention body variations like tall, short, fat, skinny, and so on. And this variety of sizes, shapes, and colors is something that is so normal to our American experience that we don't even notice it.

In fact, within my immediate family we have blue eyes, brown eyes, hazel eyes, light skin (the kind that sizzles in the sun), olive skin, blonde hair, brown hair, red hair, and my own RTG hair (for all you acronym-phobic Luddites out there, RTG hair is "Rapidly Turning Gray").

But after just a few days in Japan, I found myself startled any time I spotted someone who was more than about five feet, seven inches tall or who had anything other than black hair and brown eyes. Someone told me that out of the millions of people living in the general vicinity of Saga, there were something like twenty-seven foreigners.

What I find even more amazing than that fact is the idea that somebody would even know it – in parts of rural America nobody has any idea from one day to the next how many Mexicans might be living out behind the barn.

As invited foreigners in Japan, we were treated with great kindness and respect. We stayed with a Buddhist monk and his family who took us in warmly, as if we were oversized and slightly dull-witted family members.

But it was always clear, in ways that went way beyond mispronouncing the simplest Japanese words and bashing our heads on the tops of door frames, that we were not the kind of people their world was designed for. For example, they would stare in open-mouthed amazement at the sheer quantities of raw fish and seaweed we could consume, and they had an intense clinical interest in my "big biru bella."

For those few of my readers who are not completely conversational in Japanese, "biru" is "beer," one of the first and most useful Japanese words I learned. "Bella" apparently refers to that part of the American physique found just above (and sometimes flopping over) the belt buckle.

The Japanese also have a very different sense of personal history than we do. Chaiko, our hostess, showed us a small shrine which pays specific tribute to the lives of at least the last seven generations of Buddhist monks in her husband's family line. It seems like they can trace ancestors back to the stone age, while I think a lot of Americans would be really hard-pressed to come up with their grandparents' middle names.

So there it is. In the past four weeks I've told you everything you need to know before you go to Japan and try to make people understand what you're saying by repeatedly shouting it and using a Charlie Chan accent.

Next week – something completely different.

And Then There's Football

Well, Thanksgiving is behind us. We're still a couple of weeks away from having all our footwear caked with that festive white halo of parking lot salt and all our credit cards maxed out. This means that I have a little time to talk about another thing that happens a lot this time of year – football.

Where I live, the whole football fan thing is pretty much winding down for the year. The University of Michigan has polished off the worst season in the school's history, so instead of preparing for any sort of appearance in a post season bowl game the young student-athletes are back in their dorms, probably concentrating on their dissertations in existentialist literature or chemical thermodynamics.

Our local professional football guys, the Detroit Lions, are well on their way to cementing a place in the pantheon of sports legends as the worst team in NFL history. If they lose their next two games they will tie the current champions, the 1976 Tampa Bay Buccaneers, at 0-14. Just two more losses after that, well within the reach of this inspired Detroit squad, and they will set a record that can only be beaten if the NFL should someday go to a 17 game season.

So I guess we still do have something to root for.

Even without a fan connection, I've been tuning in on some football games over the past couple of weekends, and watching them brought back some fond memories. You see, I played a little football when I was too young to clearly understand the meaning of the words "compound fracture," so I thought I'd take this opportunity to share a few thoughts about the game.

The first thing to understand about football is that it is a game of inches. This means that a player who stands 6'8" inches tall can smash a player who is a mere 8" shorter (like me) into a sort of lumpy pulp with a helmet and shoulder pads mixed in.

Another important thing every player must learn is that psychology is probably your most important weapon. Before the play, you have to look across (and up) at the opposing player with a confident sneer. The idea is to intimidate him, to let him know that you are not afraid of him.

In fact, it is better if you actually show scorn for him. Insult him. Say something derogatory about his mother. Call his sister nasty names. Tell him that those stretchy football pants make him look fat. And then when the ball is snapped, you must explode across the line and hit him with all the uninhibited violence you can muster.

Later, when you regain consciousness in the emergency room, you will have the satisfaction of knowing that you played the game as it was meant to be played.

There were some types of football games that I always thought were a lot more fun than others to play in. My favorite was when heavy rain would turn a natural turf field into a big muddy Slip 'N Slide with yard markers. For one thing, every time the 6'8" guy and four or five of his friends fell on me, my body would just squish down into the muck. Sometimes I would even kind of squirt out from under the pile, like that big old glob of guacamole and chicken does when you slam your fist down on an overloaded fajita.

The best part of playing in the mud was that picking the clumps of sod out of my face mask and my teeth gave me a great way to while away the time on the bench.

Of course, to be absolutely clear, I should point out that what I am talking about here is good old American football, not the European kind. European "football" involves a lot of skinny guys in shorts prancing around on a big field and kicking a white ball back and forth. Eventually one player happens to brush against the jersey of an opponent, at which point the opponent whose jersey was brushed falls to the ground and writhes in agony until his team gets a free kick.

At least I think that's how it goes…

A Case of Classical GAS

As anyone who has been around me at all is aware, I play the guitar. I play it constantly, enthusiastically, and just well enough that I usually avoid being attacked by angry villagers with pitchforks. And for 38 years I had one main guitar, born the same year as me, a 1951 Martin.

I picked up that guitar when I was in college. I traded for it, swapping all the stuff I had left over from my 1960's "rock star" days - including a solid body electric guitar that would be worth a small fortune today – for a little wooden box that had pick marks on the top and "John S. Miracle, WCPM, Middlesboro, Kentucky" stenciled on the guitar case. It seems that old John had spent about 20 years breaking it in, and I decided that it was the least I could do to carry on in his honor.

I hardly ever went anywhere without my guitar, and I wasn't shy about hauling it out and banging through some songs with a bunch of friends. I can think of at least a few times over the years when that guitar and I woke up on a beach somewhere, both of us sleeping off what was probably a pretty interesting night before.

Like me, as the years went by my old guitar got a little banged up - everything still worked pretty well, considering, but there were a couple of dings on the fenders.

And that was just the way I liked it. For the last decade or so that guitar always sat in a stand next to my computer, so that whenever I needed to sit back and figure out how to unscramble some ungodly mess I had just written, I could grab it and hammer out a few bars of "Little Martha" to clear my head.

A couple of years ago when I began playing on stage a lot for Lost Voices, it became apparent that my old guitar was hurting. It would no longer play in tune, and the strings were sawing my fingers off. It turns out that it was way overdue for some expensive neck repair that I didn't have the cash to pay for.

So I did the smart thing - I sold my guitar to a collector, picked up a spotless 10-year-old guitar that was in perfect condition and ready for the stage, and put a fair amount of money in the bank.

Well, in this case "smart" didn't work out all that well for me. The first problem I had with the new guitar is that I just could not get comfortable playing it. It was designed with a special slim neck and super fast action, and I was used to playing on a neck that had been, charitably speaking, hacked by hand out of a small tree trunk.

A bigger problem, though, was that this guitar was the most beautiful thing I ever saw. It had snowflake and rosette inlays, specially selected and matched woods, premium finishes, and not a scratch on it anywhere. I was afraid to get it out of the case.

And so, after a year of trying to adapt, I decided to sell that gorgeous guitar and get a more simple one with a beefier neck, one that I wouldn't be afraid to put a few pick marks on. I spent hours reading guitar reviews and haunting the online forums for guitar fanatics. I combed eBay and Craigslist and all the other guitar buy/sell Web sites.

And somewhere in that process I picked up a major case of what the guitar fanatics call "GAS" – Guitar Acquisition Syndrome. This means that I've been eating, sleeping, and dreaming about nothing but buying guitars. I remember when I used to eat, sleep and dream about nothing but playing them.

After a couple of months of this, I have finally hit pay dirt - I just completed a deal for a guitar that seems to suit me perfectly. With a little luck, I intend to keep this one and spend the rest of my life wearing a hole right through the top of it. I have to admit, though, it was pretty darned fun to look at all the cool guitar pictures in those "For Sale" ads and dream.

But I guess that, deep down, what I really dream of is someday coming up with a big pile of money, so that maybe John S. Miracle and I can go find that collector and get our guitar back.

All Things Considered, I'll Stick With My RTG Hair

A few weeks ago I described my hair color as "RTG." This, of course, stands for Rapidly Turning Gray, and is a matter of pride for me.

Now I'm not talking about "sexy gray," like Richard Gere or Anderson Cooper. Their gray hair is more of a fashion statement. In fact, I think those guys were salt-and-pepper in about the third grade, and I'm pretty sure they used that "silver fox" thing to charm the third grade chicks right out of their Twinkies.

No, I'm talking about the gray hair you get because you are old. Now, I have been working on getting old for a very long time. And through all those years I have filled most of my leisure hours with pastimes like scuba diving under frozen lakes, so I feel like I have pretty much earned every patch of white that has cropped up on my noggin.

In other words, rather than resisting the signs of all those passing years, I'm just plain happy to still be here.

Some guys do not agree with me on this. At the recent Rock And Roll Hall Of Fame induction ceremony, a dark-haired inductee named Dave Clark (from the 1960s British Invasion band the Dave Clark Five) smiled and waved at the cameras, flanked by two guys who appeared to be his grandfathers – bass guitarist Rick Huxley, and lead guitarist Lenny Davidson. Since they all knew each other in high school, I suspect old Dave might have had a little work done.

Of course, Iggy Pop, who will be 61 years old this April, also appeared on that Rock Hall Of Fame show, shirtless and without any sign of gray hair. I'm told that the secret in his case is that David Bowie had Iggy embalmed sometime in the mid 1970s.

Women have always waged a pitched battle against the signs of age by coloring their hair. Fluctuations from blonde to brunette have apparently exposed Rock Hall Of Fame inductee Madonna to so many toxic chemicals over the years that the girl, born and raised in Michigan, has been left with a debilitating British accent.

But I think the overall issue here is that most women fight this particular war a lot better than most guys do. They spend long hours and hundreds of dollars having experts color their hair, carefully blending colors and adding highlights to achieve that "natural look."

Most guys, on the other hand, spend about seven bucks and seven minutes in the shower with a bottle of Grecian Formula attempting to recapture their lost youth. Rather than achieving any sort of a "natural look," they wind up sporting more of a "black dog-fur helmet" motif.

A few years ago my friend Megan convinced me that I would look a lot better if I would let her give me a few blonde highlights to sort of disguise the gray. Ignoring the clearly flashing danger sign that she and a bottle of Clairol had already teamed up to make my wife look like Cher, I calmly read a book while Megan worked her magic.

The only further comment I care to make about that particular episode in my life is that, all things considered, bright flaming orange is probably not the best color for me.

So I guess the bottom line here is that now I just want to go gracefully into my golden years. Besides, Megan just told me that if I had a nose job and a little work done around my eyes, I would look a little bit like Richard Gere…

…And I Can't Find My Way Home

Hey, news flash! I have a GPS in my cell phone!

Now, my guess is that your response to that opening will pretty much sort you out by age. If you are under about thirty, it was probably, "Well, duh!" If you are anywhere between thirty and fifty, the chances are you said to yourself, "Interesting. Maybe mine does too. I think I'll go check." And if you're around my age, over fifty, you probably were thinking something like, "Geeze, I don't remember applesauce giving me so much gas!"

For those of you who are not real familiar with this bit of twenty-first century technology, a GPS is a device that can show you exactly where you are on the planet. And, if you let it know where you want to go, it can tell you how to get there.

Kind of like a map, only it makes an odd sort of "crunching" sound if you fold it up wrong.

My first GPS experience was a couple of years ago, with one built into the dashboard of my brother's car. At that time, integrated GPS systems were not as common as they are now. But since my brother has never owned a car that was less technologically advanced than an F-18, I was not particularly surprised to see the very latest equipment staring back at me from just north of the surround-sound stereo.

I was surprised, however, at how cool the thing was. My brother programmed in our trip - an operation the details of which I largely missed because I was busy playing with the power windows - and we were off. As we rolled along, it was kind of like watching a Pac Man game. A little rectangle, presumably our vehicle, sat in the middle of the screen, while the street, presumably the one we were on, scrolled past under us. I could see the side streets and the cross streets all around us, but there did not seem to be any of those little ghost-thingies or smiley faces eating dots anywhere.

And then the GPS started talking to us. "Turn left, one quarter mile," it would say in a calm female voice. Then, in a little less than a quarter of a mile she would weigh in again with "Turn left, two hundred feet." And then, at exactly the right moment, "Turn left now."

After we made our turn, the GPS did not bother to congratulate us. Sticking strictly to business she immediately said, "Now proceed straight for seven miles." This went on for quite a while, until I was beginning to consider the GPS a friendly and knowledgeable traveling companion. Good old "G."

The problem came when my brother, who had driven to our destination at least a thousand times and knew every inch of the trip blindfolded, decided to take a shortcut to beat some traffic. As he turned off the highway, "G" said calmly, "Incorrect turn."

My brother ignored her and kept on going. "Incorrect turn," she said, and I was sure I could hear her voice rising slightly. "Go back now!"

This kept up for a while, and I could tell "G" was getting upset. After she said, "For the love of God, please go back! I'm begging you!" I said to my brother, "You know, maybe we should go back. She seems to know what she's talking about."

Instead, he switched "G's" power off, turned on the radio, and drove us blissfully on toward our destination.

Then, about a year ago, my wife and I were in Pittsburgh for my nephew's wedding. Since

Pittsburgh is a notoriously difficult city to navigate in, and since I've been known to get lost in a good-sized bathroom, my brother loaned me a portable GPS he happened to have with him.

The first time I tried to use it, I immediately wished that during my previous encounter I had not been quite so fascinated with those power windows. This one didn't talk, but I spent a lot of time poking buttons and looking at messages like "Acquiring satellite," or "Your desired destination is in Bangkok, Thailand – Y/N?"

At one point I thought I had it dialed in and operating until, trying to go from one point to another in downtown Pittsburgh, we wound up in what I'm pretty sure was just outside of Hog Knuckle, Tennessee.

At least, having driven all over western Pennsylvania while watching the GPS and trying to avoid falling off a mountain or running over a sexy dancing welder (that's a Flashdance reference – you older folks can explain it to the kids), I figured out why they call the thing a "GPS." It stands for "Going Pathetically Slow."

Interestingly, when we were in Japan, where drivers are completely unfamiliar with the concept of "slow," I noticed that every car has a combination GPS/TV gizmo positioned next to the steering wheel. Japanese drivers might occasionally consult the GPS to find their way around, but they mostly use it in TV mode to watch game shows while they are driving. I think this is to keep their minds off the fact that they are careening toward oncoming traffic down a two-way street that is about eighteen inches narrower than two cars side-by-side.

And now I've discovered that I have my very own GPS, built right into my cell phone. I'm excited! I think I'll learn how to use it – right after I figure out how to turn off that Debbie Boone "You Light Up My Life" ring tone.

I Still Can't Find My Way Home

Last week I wrote about my experience with GPS technology. Well, I heard from quite a few readers who had similar stories to share, along with one person who wanted to inform me that GPS does not stand for "Going Pathetically Slow." It seems the device is actually named in honor of Gwendolyn Peabody Snuffbox, who was a key member of a research team responsible for developing something they liked to call a "global positioning system."

I stand corrected. I also received this comment:

I enjoyed reading about your experience with the GPS, but I have to say that it serves you right. Why can't you just navigate the old fashioned way – with MapQuest?

Signed, A Traditionalist

Well, Traditionalist makes a pretty good point; sometimes the ways of our forefathers can be the best in the long run. MapQuest, along with its cousin Google Maps, can indeed provide any potential pioneer with a map and turn-by-turn directions from driveway to destination.

I've just discovered that with Google Street View, you can even print out pictures of what you will see through your windshield at various key points along the trip. You will know your exit is coming up when you see the National Rifle Association's "Jesus Loves Semi-Automatic Assault Weapons" billboard to your right, and a white panel truck towing a riding lawn mower on a green trailer in the lane ahead of you.

There are only two things wrong with using MapQuest or Google Maps. First, to use them you have to think ahead and plan your trip. Does anyone else remember their parents ordering the old AAA TripTik six weeks before it came time to throw the suitcases and hula hoops in the trunk of the old Fairlane and head off for Disneyland? Well, this is exactly the same thing - except it takes about thirty seconds online. Still, it's the principle of the thing.

The second problem is that the directions are not always totally accurate. On several occasions I've had my MapQuest printout leave out just one little turn I was supposed to make. As much as I'd like to be charitable and say, "Well hey, they almost got it right," you have to resent those unplanned two-hour side trips to Botkins, Ohio.

Some couples, where at least one spouse is a born navigator, have it made when it comes to traveling. You've seen these people, cool and confident, cruising down the highway with a large compass on the dashboard and a map casually unfolded across the passenger's lap. I can just hear the conversation; "Reduce speed one third and come about to course two-two-zero, honey. I want to stop up ahead there for some beef jerky and a Diet Coke."

My wife and I are not so fortunate. I'm the first to admit that I have spent a good part of my traveling life wondering if someone was moving whole towns around just to confuse me. And my wife can actually sit watching a sunset without having any idea what direction she is facing.

So when we travel we need all the help we can get. We were thinking that maybe we should invest in a really good GPS and then learn how to use it. But just to keep us on our toes, I think it would be fun to get one that had a little bit of New York attitude;

"Ok Doofus, your turn is coming up at the next light. You think you can maybe handle a left without spilling your latté?"

Now that's navigation!

Who Were They?

I have the privilege of coaching several creative writing groups, two of which are made up of middle and high school students. These are kids who are as incredibly gifted as they are depressingly young and cool.

A couple of weeks ago, I gave the kids a writing prompt. They were to imagine a very old man or woman sitting alone in a wheel chair or on a park bench, then write a story, poem or vignette asking the question, "Who was I?" I wanted them to look well past even the advanced years of their creative writing coach, so they wouldn't get hung up on the fact that I dress and speak weird, or that I increasingly seem to have brown spots on my skin and hair sprouting in unfortunate places.

What gave me this idea was an encounter with a man I've known casually for some time.

He wrote and self-published a rather good book expressing his gentle philosophy, and he is always interesting to talk to.

Whenever I can make the time.

You see, he is right around the age my father would be if he were still alive, and sort of frail, and I don't think his hearing is all that great. Sometimes it takes a fair amount of repeating and rephrasing to have a conversation with him, and with all the important things I have going on in my life, it doesn't always fit into my schedule.

When I saw him a few weeks ago, I was busy, on my way to do something critical - like check my email, or recharge my iPod, or jot down an idea for a new dog poo joke. So I just said, "hi" to him and flew along on my way.

He smiled and returned my greeting, probably thinking it would be nice to chat for a few minutes. But he was way too considerate to slow down a mover-and-shaker like me in the midst of full-on moving and shaking.

I noticed as I dashed by that he was wearing a World War II Veteran's cap, with his branch of the service proudly embroidered on it. It looked brand new, and I couldn't help thinking that he probably received it as a Christmas gift from a grandchild - who might be only vaguely aware that there even was such a thing as World War II.

In all the conversations we have had, this man has never mentioned the War or that he had any involvement in it.

A little later, as I checked my email, recharged my iPod, and wrote my dog poo joke, I couldn't escape the thought that this little man, who looks so delicate that a good stiff breeze could sweep him into the air like just another dried-up oak leaf in autumn, was really a whole lot more than he appeared to be.

Did he wade ashore at Normandy? Did he ride a tank in the deserts of North Africa? Did he dodge the bullets of a jungle sniper on a tiny Pacific island? Did he shiver in a foxhole in Bastogne? Could his less-than-perfect hearing date back to the roar of the giant guns of a great battle ship?

Might he have seen the man standing next to him literally torn apart by the fury of war, only to spend the years since that moment wondering why he was spared and that man was not?

After the War, did he help build the highways that tie our nation together? Did he have a hand in conquering some of the diseases that once made simply growing up a pretty iffy proposition? Was he involved in inventing and building the technology that has changed just about everything about who we are and how we talk to each other?

And did he raise a family, hoping that all the struggles of his life might add up to a world in which his grandchildren could be happy and healthy, in which they could buy their grandpa a hat for Christmas without knowing firsthand just how much honor and courage went into that hat?

You know, the next time I see this quiet, modest, fragile little man, I think I should probably just go ahead and let the battery in my iPod run down.

We All Fall Together – Ten Sure Signs That Summer is Over

On Sunday, September 23, we experienced the magnificent Autumnal Equinox, one of the two days out of every year when we enjoy exactly equal amounts of day and night. It also marks the beginning of Autumn, or Fall, the favorite season of football fans and leaf rake manufacturers.

The other day of the year with exactly twelve hours of daylight is the Vernal Equinox, which, of course, marks the coming of Verne.

The onset of Fall means different things to each of us. To parents it means that the kids are going back to school, to learn, to grow, and to develop eventually into happy, productive, well-educated citizens of our great land. To kids it means struggling to stay awake through Social

Studies, then having the big kid in your gym class administer your bi-weekly wedgie.

On the lake it means that over the course of the Summer the seagulls (often affectionately referred to around here as "winged rats") have deposited so much crap on every horizontal surface that even they won't sit in it any longer.

And so, working on the Standard Columnist Assumption that none of my readers are observant enough to have noticed the word "September" on their calendars or remember that they recently had to buy their kid a protractor and a new backpack, it's time for me to bring you yet another list:

Ten Sure Signs That Summer is Over.

1. The lady who walks her dog past your house every morning shows up wearing a jacket, hat and mittens, even though the air temperature is 85 degrees and she has a plume of steam rising from her collar.

2. You just saw four yellow jacket wasps abandon a dumpster full of caramel apple cores and carry away a Rottweiler.

3. The center aisles at your Costco store have blown right past Halloween, Thanksgiving and Christmas, and gone straight to their gala St. Patrick's Day displays.

4. You're wearing socks to work.

5. You're wearing socks to bed.

6. You're wearing socks.

7. You bought a brand new six-pack of sunscreen on the closeout table at the drug store but you haven't cracked it open, since nobody in your hemisphere has seen the sun in weeks.

8. You decide that there's no longer any point in properly repairing those two broken dock sections you duct-taped together last spring, since you'll just be taking it all out in a few weeks anyway.

9. You decide that there's no longer any point in putting the Christmas decorations back in the attic, since you'll just be putting them all up in a few months anyway.

10. Your baseball team didn't make the playoffs, so you're looking for another way to facilitate naps. Fortunately, you've got at least another month of PGA Golf and NASCAR - and then Professional Bowling kicks in...

How Not to Pardon a Turkey, and Other Thoughts About Thanksgiving

Ah, November in Michigan. The autumn leaves are all gone, and the ice is forming on the lake around the dock poles I was planning to get out of the water on the next nice day. Christmas decorations and the latest crop of toys have been torturing kids riding around in Costco shopping carts since Labor day. A light and festive dusting of snow is on the lawn mower.

It's Thanksgiving time!

One of the first signs of Thanksgiving is the annual Pardoning of the Turkey by various American heads of state. We all remember a few years ago when President Bush was repaid for his official act of mercy, live on national television, with an impromptu pecking by the pardoned poultry of the president's crotchical region.

In case you missed it, this year the Pardoning of the Turkey by the governor of Alaska set a whole new standard of "Maybe I should have thought this whole thing through a little more thoroughly." After she read her Commutation of Sentence proclamation to the lucky bird, she conducted a spunky on-camera interview while a turkey farm worker stood immediately behind her, staring at the camera and stuffing live non-pardonees into a beheading machine.

The word is that Governor Palin is now reconsidering her plan to go on the air in December to sing Christmas carols with her children Bristol, Piper, Track (via satellite from Iraq), Willow, and Trig, along with their cousins Mitten, Screwdriver, Lamp, Faucet, Sticker, Tampon, and Crank, while Todd stands in the background tossing puppies into a wood chipper.

Along with turkeys and unfortunate press events, Thanksgiving also serves as a reminder that the Christmas holidays are bearing down on us like a runaway team of angry reindeer. For a lot of people over the age of, say, eight, this raises a fair amount of anxiety. We feel an obligation to provide our families with a holiday season that is as magical as the ones we remember from when we were under the age of, say, eight - a wonderland of twinkle lights and youthful avarice.

We want to shower our families with all the spiritual bliss that money can buy.

Back here in Michigan we've had a pretty rough time over the past couple of weeks. The Michigan State football team got blown off the field in Happy Valley, the University of Michigan has racked up the worst football season in the history of the school, and the Detroit Lions at 0-10 are... well, they're the Detroit Lions.

Oh yeah, and the entire American automobile industry is threatening to crash and burn.

So while this Christmas deal can be pretty stressful in the best of times, this year, with our 401K plans bursting into flames and all of our credit cards checking into rehab, the season is shaping up to be downright terrifying.

Now I can't control the things I can't control, like whether Citigroup declares a shareholder dividend, or if whoever thought of marketing the Hummer gets his freaking head examined, but I can control how I'm going to think about it.

And I've decided not to participate in the recession.

My family is going to get together for Thanksgiving to have our own version of a feast. We will take some time to see and touch and talk with each other, and some more time to phone the ones we can't be with. And we will take some time to remember the ones we can't physically see or touch or talk with any longer.

Then we are going to brainstorm about how we can make each other happy this Christmas without spending a lot of money. I have no idea what we will come up with, but I feel pretty confident that it might involve the gift of seeing and touching and talking to each other. That is something the Dow Jones just can't touch.

Happy Thanksgiving!

Thanksgiving at Patrick's House

Well, the first leg of the Holiday Triathlon – Thanksgiving, Christmas and New Year - is over. As usual, my family spent a wonderful Thanksgiving day eating way too much food, drinking what some of us consider just about the right amount of beer, and trying to ignore the score of the Detroit Lions' game. The only difference this year is that we did all this, for the first time ever, at my son Patrick's house.

I would like to just make sure that you have the whole picture here. This is the same Patrick who considers Slim Jims an essential food group. He drinks milk straight from the bottle. He eats his soup with a serving spoon, right out of the sauce pan. And if he happens to think of crumbling crackers into that soup, he sends a press release to Food and Wine Magazine.

I know this, because he learned all these things from me. So when he volunteered to host Thanksgiving dinner, I was a little bit surprised.

"I'm a little bit surprised," I quipped.

"Don't worry," he said, "I'll take care of every detail. You and Mom can just show up and eat. Oh, and if you think about it, maybe you could throw your turkey fryer in the car. And some oil. And some stuffing. And a can of cranberry sauce. And whatever you need to make a pumpkin pie. Oh yeah, and a turkey."

Then the big day arrived. While Patrick's girlfriend and my wife planned the menu and tried to figure out if there were enough pickle forks and radish plates on hand, Patrick and I spent Thanksgiving morning in the really critical final preparation – installing a new set of surround-sound speakers and a subwoofer on his television so the East Ferretspleen High School Marching Band's rendition of "Up, Up and Away" at the Macy's Thanksgiving Day Parade could blow the windows out of the neighbor's garage.

Now in our family we like to deep fry our turkeys. We think that there is just something really festive about injecting and caking a huge bird with Cajun seasonings, then dropping it into a vat of peanut oil heated to a temperature just slightly greater than that of molten lava.

The only downside I've ever found to frying a turkey is that you don't get any gravy, unless you want to mix milk and flour with nine gallons of plasma-hot peanut oil. My wife solves this problem by chopping up and pan-frying the bird's "giblets" – the heart, liver, gizzard and neck – and making gravy from that. This is a perfect solution for us hearts-and-gizzards-and-other-disgusting-internal-organ-eating types, but maybe not absolutely ideal for people less inclined to culinary adventure. Oh well.

Our Thanksgiving dinner turned out great. The turkey was perfect, the conversation was stimulating, the thirty pounds of mashed potatoes were a balm to our Irish souls, and we never did tell Patrick's girlfriend how we made the gravy. Then, after dinner, as we all sat around the living room slipping in and out of food comas and listening to his new sound system broadcasting Alice's Restaurant to the Space Shuttle, I realized that my son had become a man.

And I was reminded of the first time I hosted Thanksgiving dinner, in an old converted church near Boston where I lived with Alice and Ray and Arlo, and we all had a meal that couldn't be beat, and then after dinner we took all the garbage to the dump, but the dump was closed…

Zzzzzzzzzzzz.

Wonder Where You're Going When You're 21?

Earlier this week I had the opportunity to present Lost Voices to a national conference of a group who call themselves JJET – Juvenile Justice Educators and Trainers. These are professionals from all over the country who train people to work with troubled boys and girls who have gotten themselves on the wrong side of the law.

In case you are not familiar with Lost Voices, it's an amazing program for at-risk youth that I've had the opportunity to be involved with. In it, I team up with roots music artists like Kitty Donohoe and Josh White Jr. to help the kids translate their thoughts, hopes and fears into folk and blues music. Then we help them stage a concert to perform their music for the world.

I conducted a workshop at the conference, in which all the attendees went through the same song writing process I use in the Lost Voices programs. We started with a brainstorming session, with the participants throwing out anything that happened to be on their minds to be considered as potential song themes.

I wasn't particularly surprised that what quickly surfaced as their dominant thought was the kids. After all, these are people who have dedicated their lives to the business of trying to rescue young people who have lost their way. They are all deeply caring and sensitive individuals.

What I did find striking was the way they expressed their feelings. Here's the beginning of the song they wrote:

> *Wonder where you're going when you're 21?*
> *When you don't have a dad who is missing his son*
> *Been living in a place where nobody comes*
> *Wonder if you'll live to be someone.*
> *You're hungry for a dad to see your game*
> *Who will stand up in the crowd*
> *and shout your name*
> *Hungry for a man to say,*
> *"That's my kid!"*

Right there - "Hungry for a man to say, 'That's my kid!'" - is the refrain for the entire song. What better way is there to describe the issue that lies at the heart of the struggle many of these children are going through?

It occurs to me that I have been unbelievably lucky as a father. You see, I was always able to stand up in the crowd for my son. I had the opportunity to watch him portray a singing turnip (or something like that) in the second grade pageant, and to coach his hockey teams. I was around to teach him how to water ski, and how to shave, and how to tie a neck tie. I was there to snap pictures of him looking embarrassed in his cap and gown when he graduated from high school.

I made lots and lots of mistakes along the way, and I was far from the perfect dad, but at least my son always knew that I was around and that I loved him. Now he has turned out to be a fine young man, with a college degree and a good job, and he's beginning to consider starting a family of his own.

Then I think about the kids I've worked with through Lost Voices. Each one has traveled a different road to wind up in the juvenile justice system, and each one has to travel his or her own, often rough, road back into the world. They want to find their way, but they just can't do it without help.

And there at the JJET conference I was surrounded by people who go to work each day and try to give them that help. They endure the emotional roller coasters, the joys and disappointments and successes and tragedies that go with the job. I could see that, along with all the sophisticated rehabilitation and treatment techniques they bring to their work, they bring another, very fundamental, tool.

You see, they are also willing to stand up for these struggling young people and say, in their own way, "Those are my kids."

Christmas Decorations: Finding the True Meaning of the Holidays in a Glow-In-The-Dark Plastic Reindeer

You know, I'm willing to bet that there's some guy in your neighborhood whose roof is literally sagging under the weight of a giant Santa, a small herd of reindeer, and a life-sized nativity scene – complete with "lowing" cattle, a couple of shepherds who look pretty nervous to be stapled to those roof shingles, a trio of really strung-out Magi, and a fiberglass Holy Family with the infant Messiah lit up by a 450-watt halogen bulb stuck right up his manger.

The guy who owns this house is my personal hero – I love Christmas decorations!

Yes, I called them "Christmas" decorations, not "Holiday Decorations," or any other godless secular nonsense. You see, I have a deep reverence for the collection of mostly Druid, Viking and Pagan traditions that today form the Hallmark® of this holiest of all seasons.

As the Apostle Paul (probably) said, "Yea, verily shall we cometh together and praise His coming with feasting and rejoicing and Midnight Madness Sales, for the angels of the Lord did proclaim tidings of great comfort and seasonal retail activity. Though the actual birth of our Savior was, if I recalleth correctly, sometime in March, or maybe April – no, it was in March I'm pretty sure – remembereth that one time we didst throw him a party and he didst act all embarrassed and even a little vengeful about it? Well, I remember that it was still cold out, because, yea, was I still wearing my winter cloak, so it must have been March. Anyway, verily shall we actually celebrate in December because otherwise our rejoicing wouldst crowdeth Easter merchandising, plus what the hecketh, thou already havest thy winter solstice parties that we couldst piggyback on..." *Paul's Letter to the Petersons, 6:23.*

One big reason I love Christmas decorations is that without them, this time of year is just so incredibly dark. December 21 is officially the shortest day of the year, giving us, if my figures are correct, about eleven minutes of actual daylight. Admittedly a twinkle light doesn't throw off a whole lot of candle power, but cover the trees, bushes, and the front of a three bedroom split-level with them, and just walking by you could get yourself a pretty good twinkle tan.

I'm also crazy about the inflatables that have started showing up in the last few years. Show me a yard jammed fence-to-shed with giant vinyl elves and snowmen, and I'll show you somebody who's facing the new year looking at a major cash-back bonus on his Discover card.

Of course, my favorite holiday tradition of all is the Christmas tree. No matter what church's collection basket you prefer to drop your IOUs into, there really is something sacred about dragging a plastic blue spruce into the living room then decorating it with Gordian wads of lights and ornaments that have been packed away in the attic in dog-eared cardboard boxes held together with duct tape and marked "XMAS" in festive green magic marker. Every year for the thirty years we've been married, my wife and I have talked about trashing all the old Christmas junk and doing a trendy designer tree with all new color-coordinated lights and ornaments.

And then I spot the ragged miniature stocking with my name on it that my mother made for me when I was about four.

And the glass ornaments that my father loved when he was alive, so scratched and faded that you can no longer tell what the original color was, but each one has one part that is not all that bad, so I always turn the little tin collars that hold the hooks so the not-all-that-bad-parts show.

And the tattered little elves knitted over pipe cleaners, holding tiny pipe cleaner candy canes that my wife found in some craft shop years before we met. And the dozens of "Baby's First Christmas" ornaments that I still insist on using every year since I don't have any that say, "Baby's Twenty-Sixth Christmas."

And the little brass cash register I got for my wife when she opened her store, and the little attaché case she got for me when I started wearing a suit to work, and the little ceramic hockey player skating on a Wheaties box that Santa brought for our son when he made his first travel team.

Ok, so maybe we don't have a fifty-foot inflatable camel loaded with bags of glow-in-the-dark myrrh staked out by the mailbox. And I guess we're just too cheap to spring for the pre-programmed Star of Bethlehem Laser Light Show In-A-Box. But every year all the old junk that we do have comes out of the boxes and goes up on the tree, and it always seems to look pretty good to us.

Because it's our junk.

When The Lake Freezes Over

Our lake finally froze.

Actually, this year we had the earliest hard freeze I can remember, followed by a complete January thaw. You know, it seems like everywhere you look, the weather is doing strange things – Midwestern tornados for Christmas, winter droughts, fires, floods.

But I guess you have to respect our nation's leaders when they say the jury is still out on the cause of all this. I mean, how can we really be sure that dumping millions of tons of industrial crap into the air will upset nature's balance? And while we're studying the problem, how can we possibly justify making rash changes that might save a few thousand species at the risk of jeopardizing the ability of energy company executives to keep using platinum dental floss?

But this column is not about all that stuff. It's about ice skating.

When my son was younger, I coached his ice hockey teams. This meant that several mornings every week, at about 5 AM, I would join a bunch of other dads carrying our lifeless little bundles of kids across frozen parking lots and into the rink, stuffing them into miniature hockey pads and skates, then shoving them out on the ice.

Playing hockey on a Zamboni-groomed indoor rink is great. You always have decent ice, the lines and nets are regulation, and you have those Plexiglas-topped walls to smash into when you want to scare your mom. You have benches where you can sit between shifts and have squirt-fights with the water bottles. And afterward, there's usually juice boxes and brownies in the locker room, so you can have a food fight while you're taking your skates off.

Skating on a frozen lake, you have to watch out for cracks, uneven spots, and the occasional jet ski embedded in the ice. If you're not careful, your puck can disappear into a snow bank, lost until next July when you'll stub your toe on it sticking out of the sand in the shallows.

For goals you have to use traffic cones with a 2x4 propped across them, and you have to be sure you remember to hit the brakes before you sail out of the rink and into somebody's fishing shanty. Your nose and cheeks freeze numb, and you have to take a break every now and then to warm your hands and the toes of your skates on the bonfire made from the old dock section that finally broke for good last August.

And there's nothing in this world that's more pure, uncomplicated fun.

For years I kept a rink out in front of our house, investing a few hours each day in grooming and patching my several hundred square feet of hockey heaven. I kept heavy steel snow shovels stuck in the snow bank, and I passed a decree as Lord of the Rink that all were welcome, as long as they were willing to grab a shovel and skate a couple of human Zamboni passes.

So every afternoon the whole neighborhood would know the kids were home from school by the sound of shovels scraping along the ice. Then we would listen to the snick-snick-snick of little hockey skates and the shouts of little hockey stars, until it was too dark to have any chance of seeing the puck, and all the moms were tired of keeping dinner warm.

For my teams, every Sunday was Pond Hockey at Coach's House. One Sunday the team was in a tournament that involved an early qualifying game, with the finals in the evening.

The kids came out to the lake after the morning game and skated nonstop until it was time to head back to town. Then they piled into the cars with their heads steaming in the cold air, laughing and chattering right through the ride and the process of getting their uniforms back on for the playoff game.

Which they won.

Those kids are grown and gone now. I don't have to spend all that time clearing and grooming and patching the ice any more. I've given away the big old shovels, and I'm not even sure where my clipboard, my whistle, or my bag of pucks has wandered off to.

This morning I noticed that the neighbors a couple of doors down were out on the lake clearing a little rink. Now that I think of it, their kids should be getting just about old enough for their first skates…

You know, it's going to be mighty good to hear that snick-snick-snick again.

About The Author

Mike Ball is an award-winning humorist and author of *What I've Learned... So Far,* who lives and writes on the shores of Whitmore Lake, Michigan, sharing a roof with his wife Nancy and a psychotic Siamese cat. Their home is just North of Ann Arbor, home of the University of Michigan and one of the world's most fertile breeding grounds for hippies, folk singers, and Budweiser-soaked football fans.

In addition to cranking out his weekly humor column, Mike is a musician and the founder of Lost Voices, a Michigan non-profit group that designs and implements therapeutic roots music writing and performing programs for incarcerated and at-risk youth. As the front man of the band Dr. Mike & The Sea Monkeys, he brings his columns to musical life with such crowd pleasers as "Carlson the Pissed Off Angel," "At Least I've Got Most of My Hair," and "The Colonscopy Song."

Mike has spent most of his adult life writing and producing columns, ads, brochures, slogans, songs, menus, and anything else that needed writing, including a eulogy for a dog. During the Internet Boom of the 1990s he wrote a monthly column for a national information technology-oriented human resources magazine (now there's a combination that just screams humor!) called Itrecruitermag. These pieces covered such topics as "What to Do When You Run Into Your Boss at the Career Fair" and "So, You've Been Downsized. Sucks to Be You."

In 2003 Mike won the Erma Bombeck Award, and he was a finalist for the 2011 Robert Benchley Award. *What I've Learned So Far...* is syndicated and has online readers in eleven countries (that we know of).

Mike also spent some time as a competitive pairs water skier. He and various partners won numerous awards, including the 1997 Florida State Show Ski Championship at Cypress Gardens, the 2000 Indoor World Championship, the 2002 Michigan State Expert Division Championship, and the 2002 Division II National Championship. The better-looking member of the pair shown here is the amazing Megan Atkins.